HAVE YOUR WAY

HAVE YOUR WAY

How to Make People Do What **YOU WANT**

Richie Kasper

Published by
Rupa Publications India Pvt. Ltd 2022
7/16, Ansari Road, Daryaganj
New Delhi 110002

Sales centres:
Allahabad Bengaluru Chennai
Hyderabad Jaipur Kathmandu
Kolkata Mumbai

Copyright © Richie Kasper 2022

The views and opinions expressed in this book are the author's own and the facts are as reported by him which have been verified to the extent possible, and the publishers are not in any way liable for the same.

All rights reserved.
No part of this publication may be reproduced, transmitted, or stored in a retrieval system, in any form or by any means, electronic, mechanical, photocopying, recording or otherwise, without the prior permission of the publisher.

ISBN: 978-81-291-4189-7

First impression 2022

10 9 8 7 6 5 4 3 2 1

The moral right of the author has been asserted.

Printed in India

This book is sold subject to the condition that it shall not, by way of trade or otherwise, be lent, resold, hired out, or otherwise circulated, without the publisher's prior consent, in any form of binding or cover other than that in which it is published.

CONTENTS

Introduction vii

1. Understanding What They Need (To Fulfil Your Wants) 1
2. Trust Is a Must 5
3. A Little Lying at Work (Does Nobody Any Harm) 16
4. You Have To Be the Nicest One in the Office 25
5. Magnetic Mystery 45
6. The Modern Alpha Employee 61
7. Dynamic Diplomacy 72
8. Power-Play Like a Pro 91
9. The Cunning One Climbs the Corporate Ladder 111
10. Ace Your Arguments 131

INTRODUCTION

Not getting what you want either means you don't want it enough, or you have been dealing too long with the price you have to pay.[1]

—Rudyard Kipling, English writer and journalist.

We all want something. Take a minute to think about a recent situation in which you wanted something from another person. Maybe you wanted your partner to clean the dishes, maybe you wanted a promotion from your boss or you wanted this attractive person at a party to go on a date with you. How did you really get it—assuming you got it, in the first place? Once you got it, you wanted more, didn't you?

The only truth about human nature is greed. Greed is a positive thing. Accept it. It's fantastic. It is to be lived. In fact, it's possible that greed is the only thing that can save us. Do you have any doubts? Greed is at the root of most of our development, relationships, and even nations.

Greed is beneficial not just to yourself, but also to others. You may significantly improve the lives of your family, society, and even the planet by raising your own life. Even Mother Teresa

---

[1] Rudyard Kipling, 'Rudyard Kipling Quotes', AZ Quotes, https://www.azquotes.com/quote/554451, Accessed on 4 February 2022.

was greedy. As crazy as it sounds, she had an unquenchable thirst for serving the poorest of the poor. Missionaries are greedy in their quest to spread their religious beliefs. Any successful entrepreneur is greedy. They have an insatiable desire to see their product come to market. They want to see their invention in the hands of as many people as possible. They want their book to hit *The New York Times* bestseller list. They will do *whatever it takes* to achieve their goal.

You just need to get greedy. You need to focus so intently on what it is you want that your desire seeps out of your pores; and of course, if you're greedy, you're going to want to get more and more of what you desire.

So, how do you really get what you want? In an ideal world, we could just ask for all of the things we want from people and they would comply. But the world is not perfect and we can't get everything we want by just asking or waiting for 'the Lord's mercy' or whatever your grandmother is thankful for during thanksgiving dinner. It's not God who gets you what you want—but your tactics and intelligence. So, what can you do to get what you want?

You might say you plead or ask politely. However, I say, quit showing your hands and begging. Instead, just get what you want with an intact ego. Why, you ask. Why not, right? Isn't it true that if they don't give you what you want, they're the problem? You have a blog, a product or a charity that you believe will change the world, but you can't help but be anxious, no matter how excited you are about the possibilities and how much faith you have in yourself. Ask yourself these questions:

- If you ask a popular blogger for a link, will you get a reply?
- If you ask a partner to email a product offer to their list, will they agree?
- If you ask a friend for a donation, will they write you a check?
- If you ask your boss for a leave, will they say yes?
- You don't know. You can't know. And does it bother you?

Wouldn't it be easier if you could just close your eyes, pop over into their mind and seize control? It's too bad that this isn't possible—or, is it? As it happens, mind control is possible (sort of) but that's more than enough for you to have your way.

No, you can't turn your customers, partners and in-laws into mindless zombies; but what you can do is influence them and manipulate them. In fact, there's a science to it.

Back in the 1980s, a researcher by the name of Dr Robert Cialdini wrote a book called *Influence: The Psychology of Persuasion*. He outlined different principles scientifically proven to influence people, as well as suggestions for how to do it. Cialdini calls it 'influence', but let's face it, this is just a smart power play and there's nothing wrong with that if it gets you what you want. Yes, this is a dark book—but it will surely help you get whatever you want through mind control.

Now, here's the bad news: mind control isn't about magic powers, arcane arts or even shaving your head and gallivanting around in a wheelchair (although, I've been tempted). The truth is, it's about something that makes a lot of people squeamish: some good-old hidden manipulation (not to sugar-coat it). You're probably being manipulated every day, whether you realize it or not, in both your personal and professional life. Marketers and corporations all across the world use manipulation to persuade us to buy particular items and conduct our lives in specific ways:

- Buy this brand of shoes.
- Eat more vegetables.
- Quit drinking.
- Vote for this political party.
- Go watch this new romantic comedy you honestly couldn't care less for.

The word 'manipulate', by definition, merely means 'to handle or control in a skilful manner,' or 'to control or influence a person or situation,' and has no intrinsically negative implications. So, one of these manipulation scenarios is beneficial and one is bad? Is it immoral to push individuals to stop drinking or adopt a healthier lifestyle, or can this be considered positive manipulation? (Look at me manipulating you into believing manipulation isn't bad.) My main point is—nobody sees your mind games as manipulation as long as you make them believe you're persuading them for *their* good.

You also see classic manipulation in your world leaders. It's fun to follow a leader, isn't it? They're human, yet they're Gods to us. They're all over our media, yet they're absolute mysteries: a leader who can get you all excited about a vision and the means to achieve it. It's a common human instinct. While leaders can be effective without being charismatic, having charisma—that winning combination of charm, enthusiasm and manipulation—can be a significant advantage. It's difficult to resist a captivating individual. Take, for example, Cesar Chavez. The labour and civil rights activist was a knowledgeable speaker, but it was his enthusiasm for what he was saying, combined with his ability to grasp what regular people wanted to hear (due to his charisma), that attracted so many people to his cause. Here are some other examples of leaders who were like demi-gods to the masses thanks to their masterful mind control tactics.

Napoleon Bonaparte	Despite standing just 5-feet and 2-inches tall and being mocked as a child in Corsica because he didn't speak proper French, Napoleon Bonaparte has become the iconic leader we all learn about to date. As a young officer in the French army, he was smart, aggressive and fearless. He inspired great loyalty in just about *anyone* he met. Because of these traits, Bonaparte's soldiers won numerous battles for France and, by the age of 34, he was emperor of the country in 1804.
	Bonaparte was successful because he intuitively understood a lot about human behaviour, such as the importance of thanking people who helped you succeed. Bonaparte once requested money and silver from people he captured after his troops won a decisive battle. He then gave it to his warriors as a token of his appreciation. He also learned how critical it was to gain the trust of those he wasn't in charge of. As a result, when his army invaded another country, he made it obvious to the inhabitants that he wasn't fighting them, but rather their dictator leaders. This frequently converted people into supporters, strengthening his efforts.
	Bonaparte often joined his soldiers in battle too and would do any job—even ones normally reserved for the lowest-ranking soldiers. This inspired tremendous loyalty, even for the most murderous of deeds.

Xi Jinping	Bookstores across China give prime display to his collection of speeches and essays, which has sold more than 5 million copies, according to state media. You see his statues all across the country and the Chinese kids supposedly call him 'Good Uncle Xi' even though he's a tyrant. It's safe to say Xi Jinping is a god in China. How? Due to his cult of personality. He knows exactly what his masses want to hear, what they lack and how he can trick them into believing they can get it: *through* him. See this statement made by him, for instance– 'The Communist party of China really strives for the happiness of the Chinese people.' As much as it makes you want to laugh, the Chinese masses are head-over-heels in love with Xi Jinping. And *that's* his masterful mind-control.
Adolf Hitler	Adolf Hitler wasn't a sociable person. He was a quirky kid who left school at 16 to become a painter in Vienna, at which he failed miserably. He had problems forming personal relationships and couldn't engage in any intellectual debate. Can you imagine? Yet, after joining the fascist German Workers' Party (later, the Nazi Party) in 1919, it took him *only two years* to become its leader. It was the perfect storm and Hitler took full advantage of it. The Germans had gotten thrashed in World War I and were poor, starving and humiliated by the terms of their surrender.

	In an almost religious manner, Hitler swept in preaching redemption and deliverance. He shouted against democracy, convinced Germans they were Aryans and superior to everyone else, and spoke out against well-defined foes such as communists and Jews. Tell the down-trodden what they want to hear, act like their messiah, and voila, you're their brand-new God.
	Hitler had a clear vision and was determined to convince the universe of his mission—hallmarks of a charismatic manipulator. Millions of Germans fell for it, viewing Hitler almost like a superhero or something. His staff bought the entire charade too; Hitler, surprisingly, was a kind boss, or he *pretended* to be.
	Part of Hitler's charisma was his true and utter belief that Germans were great and that he was 'the one' to lead them to take over Europe. Now, I know that everyone hates him and I know that nobody wants to be him, but we all cannot help admire his charisma. Hitler's example shows you just how powerful subtle mind control can be to achieve success and get what one wants (and yes, that doesn't mean killing people in our case).
Vladimir Putin	After he became prime minister in 1999 and president in 2000, Putin displayed an unexpected—probably even to himself—ability to appeal to his people through his self-confidence, grit and decisiveness. That is to say, he turned out to be a skilful and charismatic mind controller.

He was able to express a prevalent opinion among his people that the West had taken advantage of Russia following the fall of communism. Despite declining living standards, Putin's primary theme that the country has risen from its knees continues to connect with the majority of Russians.

In the beginning of his presidency, he indeed had very little of charisma being a rather shy person.

However, over the years, it's safe to say Putin is a demigod in the eyes of his people. His charisma is based on self-confidence, logic, moral superiority and mastery in what he does.

By 'mastery', I mean that he is capable of discussing his topics freely and consistently, always presenting a very clear and understandable line of reasoning to the audience that is hard to argue. It requires good memory for facts, being able to look at the core of any problem and the ability to build logical sequences on-the-fly. He is *excellent* at all of that. In a dialogue, he does not 'charm' opponents, nor does he 'oppress' them, but rather, he *persuades* or, if that is not possible or not required, leads the discussion so that the onlookers are persuaded of his reasoning.

This is why his favourite type of public performance is a conference—either a press-conference, a professional meeting or even an open telephone conference with the population. Yes, that's charisma for you.

What Are Some Mutual Traits of Charismatic Go-Getters and Successful Leaders?

- They recognize and compliment the strengths of others.
- They tap into the emotions of others.
- They exhibit vision and make plans.
- They understand that people want to matter.
- They identify their enemies beforehand.
- They make people feel like they have a say.
- They have passion to make things 'better' and they're great at expressing it.
- They make others believe they care about their benefits.
- They reward desired behaviours.

Wait, to make you feel a little better about picking this Machiavellian book up, let me rephrase it as *persuasion*; sounds a lot more harmless, right? There you go.

Know that persuasion is not just for salespeople and their prospects. You may be attempting to persuade an employee to improve their performance, or you may be attempting to persuade your employer to take on your wonderful idea. Your children are frequently the most effective persuaders. They seem to be born with it, whereas you, the adult, have to work hard to discover a persuasive road to success. Persuasion is all about communicating at its most fundamental level. The art of persuasion, on the other hand, is about using a sophisticated blend of communication skills and influence to persuade others to accept your ideas, recommendations or proposals once you've successfully convinced them that doing so is in their best interests, even if it's in yours. You basically make them feel they're getting what they want while, in reality, *you* are getting what *you* want.

Some economists believe that persuasion is responsible for generating one-quarter or more of America's total national income; just by persuasion, could you have imagined? Successful people in practically every profession have become those who can persuade others to act on their ideas as our economy has progressed from agrarian to industrial to knowledge-based. Consider the importance of persuasion in our daily lives:

- Entrepreneurs urge investors to invest in their new businesses.
- Job applicants encourage hiring managers to hire them.
- Politicians encourage voters to vote in their favour.
- Leaders urge people to follow certain actions plans.
- CEOs urge analysts to publish positive reports on their firms.
- Salespeople urge customers to buy their product over one offered by a competitor.
- Your wife persuades you she *needs* that diamond ring to feel good about herself.
- Your kids persuade you to let them go for that late-night rave party, even when you know they might get sloshed, high or might even get themselves killed.

Persuasion isn't an art form in the same way that painting or music are, but it does require finely tuned creative talents in language and communication. Persuasion, on the other hand, incorporates some of the characteristics of more conventional art genres. It's tough academically, sophisticated, expressive and, let's just say, crafty. You might be wondering why you should bother learning how to persuade others in the first place. Such an 'art' could even be considered wicked or manipulative. The truth is that every successful person has, at some point or another, had to persuade someone to do something in order to get what they needed or wanted. For instance, most people have to persuade an employer to hire them before they can even begin to work and earn money. Yes, what you've been doing in your job interviews all this while is, indeed, crafty persuasion.

The art of persuasion runs through many human endeavours. Salespeople convince customers to purchase goods or services. Politicians urge people to vote for them by appealing to their emotions. People are persuaded to fall for schemes and spend money they don't have by con artists. You may persuade your teacher to give you an open-book exam, persuade your girlfriend or boyfriend to marry you, or persuade someone to assist you with your volunteer programme. In fact, it's rare to find people who don't use some type of persuasion to get anything done. Let's get into some of the basics of persuasion, shall we?

Emotions vs Rationale: Who Wins?

Emotion wins. Yes, persuasion is all about emotion and then comes rationale. Indeed, we are more likely to succumb to persuasion in order to feel happy or reduce our pain rather than gaining knowledge or advance our thinking. When someone makes us feel good—intentionally or not—we will be more likely to agree with their views and be persuaded by them. Remember the last time your date made you feel great about your work and your looks, and you just couldn't get enough of them? They could practically drain you of all your wealth and you'd still want to see them because they make you feel great. *That* is the power of persuasion tapping into emotion.

In persuasion, warmth and empathy (even if it is just an act) go a lot further than logic and evidence. It is for this reason that some of our favourite ads either make us laugh, make us cry, make us want to fall in love or might even scare us for impact. That said, it is important that these attempts are subtle so that they seem genuine. Over-the-top manifestations of warmth will seem as fake, artificial and deliberately manipulative like those Super Bowl commercials with cute puppies stranded in the rain.

In short, effective persuasion targets the irrationality of human thought and desire. We may be living in a data-driven world, but that does not make people more logical. This is why the same people may regard an idea as absurd one day and amazing the next. As Arthur Schopenhauer noted: 'All truth passes through three stages. First, it is ridiculed. Second, it is violently opposed. Third, it is accepted as being self-evident.'[2]

Rationale *Does* Have a Major Role to Play

People may rely on logic or reason to achieve their goals. 'If you help me rob this bank, you will be able to feed your family,' they may tell someone (or themselves). Is there something wrong with that? When it's difficult to disagree with someone who uses reason to manipulate you, you might just give in and give the manipulator what they want. Simple.

But They Did It Too

Let's face it: we *all* compare ourselves to others. Many people use the success, attractiveness and presence of personality traits of others to gauge their own success, attractiveness, and presence of

---

[2]Arthur Schopenhauer, *The World as Will and Representation Vol 1: Volume 1*, Dover Publications Inc., 2000.

personality traits. This is something that master mind-players are well aware of. They might utilize social comparison to persuade individuals to act: 'Your co-worker does something for her partner, isn't that sweet?' 'The celebrity in the magazine in on ABC diet. You should too; it works wonders,' or perhaps, 'Sarah is so good with her presentations and she's always so punctual at work, I wonder how she does it.'

We Underestimate Others

We always feel we know best. This feeling fuels our self-deception. In line with this, we are generally more capable of spotting persuasion attempts when they are directed at others than at ourselves. Even when scientists explain this to laypeople, most still see themselves as less gullible than others—much like with other better-than-average biases. What does this mean for you? You cannot just persuade one person in the office while the others detect your ulterior motives of getting what you want—you have to charm *everyone*.

The Power of Fear

With the exception of psychopaths, the most effective way to persuade people is by tapping into their fears and insecurities. This explains why people are generally more motivated to avoid losing something they *perceive* they have (e.g., love, health, money) than gaining something they may want to have. 'Buy this and you'll live longer' is generally less effective than 'buy this or you'll die sooner.' Agreed? Thought so.

Master Manipulation Is Always Hidden

Manipulation does not always entail insulting or pressuring the other person to act in a certain way. When a mind-player utilizes self-abasement to get what they want, they will do it on purpose (even if they are the ones who are winning). You can use some good old self-abasement if you want someone to forgive you, believe you or make other efforts to strengthen their relationship with you—both at work or beyond it. That way, nobody sees you as a threat too.

Now, getting out of the world of sunshine and rainbows, the master-mind gamer knows the power of mind-control to get what they want without getting their hands dirty. They know it's the only way to the top. Being too nice only lets you down. However, playing nice leads you up the ladder. Here are some harsh truths for you:

- In the corporate jungle, you either play or get played: it's a zero-sum world—of dog eat dog.
- There is no win-win at work: in a zero-sum world full of ambitious people wanting good for themselves, there cannot be win-win.
- Relationships between equals do not exist: it's either—one wins or lose. There is more power-play in the office than you realize.
- You cannot trust others: since everyone is out to play you to surpass you at the corporate ladder, you cannot be too vulnerable. *Ever.*

Mark Twain has stated, 'It's easier to fool people than to convince them that they have been fooled.' Persuasion basically implies foolery—just a foolery that has been glossed over with icing and cherry, both in the workplace and beyond it.

So, whether you *should* learn better persuasion techniques really isn't the question. The question is *why* you haven't done so already.

I

UNDERSTANDING WHAT THEY NEED (TO FULFIL YOUR WANTS)

One of the best ways to influence people is to make them feel important. Most people enjoy those rare moments when others make them feel important. It is one of the deepest human desires.[1]

—Roy T. Bennett, author of *The Light in the Heart*

One of the earliest and most well-known theories of motivation is Abraham Maslow's. It's usually depicted as a triangle or a pyramid (I'm sorry if nasty school memories are flooding your mind right now.) It belongs to the school of motivation theories, which means that it focuses on what motivates people rather than the mechanisms by which they are driven.

The theory was developed in the 1940s, but it wasn't generally accepted until 1954. Various people have questioned the validity of some components of this model, as they do with most content models of motivation. Despite this, it is popular and has a good reputation in the corporate world. In

---

[1] Roy T. Bennett, *The Light in the Heart*, 2016.

the workplace, you may have seen it in leadership and personal development programmes.

Maslow's hierarchy of needs says that all humans share the same types of needs and that these categories of needs have a hierarchy. Loosely speaking, this hierarchy goes from the basic things we need for survival to a sense of fulfilling our potential and finding our purpose in life.

Maslow was right. As you surely know, we need to feel safe, belong, and matter once we have food and shelter, but before we may seek self-actualization (the Smart State). A person cannot enter their Smart State without these three crucial keys—they cannot perform, innovate, feel emotionally engaged, agree or go forward.

Now, what exactly do people around you crave? This is more important for you to get what *you* crave because you have to target their weak points. Safety, belonging and to matter are essential to your brain and your ability to overall perform at work, home and in life. The stronger our sense of safety, both mental and physical, the greater our sense of connection with others, or the sense that we are all in this together and belong together, the greater our sense that we personally matter, make a difference, and contribute to the larger good. The company, relationship, family, team and individual's success will all improve as a result.

In every communication, in every conflict, we are subconsciously either reinforcing or begging for safety, belonging, mattering or a combination. It's neurological or primal. There is nothing you can do to override or change this subterranean subconscious programming as much as you may try.

Security means creating an environment where we can take risks, stretch and grow. Is it safe to take risks at your company?

Being valued means that each of us contributed significantly in a unique way. We all have an impact. We are appreciated and publicly recognized. Is this how your company culture operates?

Belonging means fostering an environment in which we all feel like a close-knit tribe. We are all equal, and we are all rowing in the same direction to achieve our objectives. Consider gangs, where members will literally kill to stay in the tribe. That is how strong this condition is. Humans are biologically wired to scan the tribe to determine where they stand as a survival technique. The human brain will ask questions like these:

- As a leader, am I at the centre of the tribe, in the neutral middle or am I being pushed out or excluded from the tribe?
- Am I being recognized for what I bring to the table?
- Do others regard me favourably?

Belonging is important to humans because when we were cavemen and cavewomen living on the plains and if your tribe ousted you, your chances of survival were minimal. After all these years, our biology still works this way and you can always use that to your advantage while influencing people to give you what you want. 'This is not about being popular. It's about being valued,' Britt Andreatta, author of *Wired to Grow: Harness the Power of Brain Science to Master Any Skill,* suggests. She iterates, 'At a minimum, most of us need to know we can make a contribution—using our strengths, gifts, or talents—and what is contributed is valued by the team. They may not like me, but I am needed.' Our biological stress decreases and frees us up to do higher-level work when we can confidently say, 'Yes, I can contribute. And yes, I'm valued.'[2]

---

[2] Britt Andreatta, *Wired to Grow: Harness the Power of Brain Science to Master Any Skill*, 7th Mind Publishing, 2016.

Safety, belonging and mattering is already prevalent in your life and company. Let's see where, by doing a quick quiz. For each behaviour below, what is the person craving?

- A Fight/Flight/Freeze person craves ——
- An 'us vs them' person craves ——
- A victim-player craves ——
- An eternal recognition-seeker craves ——

What are the answers? 1. Safety, 2. Belonging, 3. Mattering, 4. Mattering. Sure, 1-4 could crave all three, but it's helpful to look at what is most essential and then to provide that. It gets results faster.

So, as a total charmer, you must identify whether it is safety, belonging and/or mattering that is most important to the people in your life and then do everything you can to make them believe you can satisfy that subterranean subconscious need. Now, memorize this powerful formula:

Safety + Belonging + Mattering = Trust

When people trust you, they believe you're doing everything for their benefit (even if it's only for your own) and go along with you, as smooth as butter. This means you must behave in ways that make people around you—at least in the professional world—feel that they are safe, that they belong and that they matter (I mean, our greedy politicians do that to us all the time.) At our emotional core, we all want safety, belonging and mattering. To influence anyone, we must influence emotionally.

2

TRUST IS A MUST

The trust of the innocent is the liar's most useful tool.[3]

—Stephen King.

As you are probably aware, gaining someone's trust is frequently the first step in persuading them of anything. We all seem to be in the persuasion game these days, 'selling' ourselves to potential employers, friends and partners.

How can you quickly and easily become a trusted adviser—someone that people will turn to for help and advice and perhaps buy things from? There's another psychological principle you can employ to quickly build trust. People who like them have a high level of trust in them. And people like people who they think are similar to them. What are some hacks for you to instantly gain trust?

Nice Guys *Don't* Finish Last; Play the Nice Guy

Likability matters. In your career, most of the opportunities will

---

[3] Stephen King, *Needful Things*, Hodder & Stoughton, 2011.

come through other people and people give opportunities to the people they like. In relationships, someone has to like you before they can love you. Anywhere in life, if people like you, they are more willing to be brainwashed—oops, I mean, *there for you*.

Consider running a business. In any business, you need to deal with people all the time: customers, suppliers, contractors, employees and peers. If your customers don't like you, they'll buy from somebody else. If your suppliers don't like you, they won't give you their best rates. If your contractors dislike you, they won't be as serious about delivering on time; same goes for your employees. You can also forget about getting help from peers who dislike you.

- People talk to people they like.
- People share information with whom they like.
- People buy from people they like.
- People are loyal to people they like.
- People refer or introduce people they like.

From every angle of human interaction, the basic question: 'Do I like this person?' is being asked. Being able to get more people to say, 'yes' to this question makes you almost invincible. Remember—the master-charmer doesn't show he's overtly charming; he plays the nice guy so he seems to be absolutely harmless. I'll get more into this in the next chapter; hang on.

Say Good Things About Others (Even If You Don't Mean a Single Word)

Tell them how much you love your sister or how well your mother cooks pasta. Tell them how much you admire your 'wonderful' boss and how you've learnt so much from them. Talk highly of your team and how well they all collaborate during a project (even if you secretly want to get rid of all of them). What does this do? This makes your target feel like you say good things about them behind their back too. It's an instant trust-gaining spell, trust me.

Open With a Bang

Research shows that most people decide whether or not they like you within the first seven seconds of meeting you. The rest of the conversation is spent internally justifying their initial reaction. This may sound terrifying, but by understanding it, you can use it to significantly improve your likeability. Positive body language is inextricably linked to first impressions. Strong posture, a firm handshake, smiling and opening your shoulders to the person you're talking to will all help you make a good first impression.

Greet the Target Warmly (Even If You Hate Seeing Their Face)

Every time you see them, greet them as if you were greeting an old friend you hadn't seen in a while (as difficult as that is). Smile deeply. After all, they're the ones who are going to give you what you want. A great smile is remembered. When you smile deeply, you improve your mood and physiology and exude warmth. A colleague told me that in his first job as a salesperson for a brokerage, he'd have to make at least 200 cold calls per day. His boss installed mirrors on their workstations. They were supposed to smile in the mirror before the call. Before every sales call, I take a quick break, breathe deeply and then smile.

Vulnerability Is a Weapon

Psychologists will often do something that makes them appear fallible—such as spilling their pencils or a cup of coffee, or telling a bad joke. 'They'll do these things to make them more approachable in a way that humanizes them and it helps to put people at ease,'[4] says Schweitzer. Telling your new coworker an embarrassing incident or going out for karaoke can do wonders for your relationship because showing vulnerability has the ability to change how someone perceives their relationship with you.

Use All Your Non-Verbal Weapons

This is a pretty simple one. You want to appear non-threatening. Smiling is the most effective nonverbal technique for appearing more accommodating. However, you can enhance your smile in a subtle way.

A slight head tilt communicates to the other person that you are at ease with them and trust them. Another nonverbal to strive for is a slightly lower chin angle. High chin angles give the impression that you're looking down at them. Body angle is another important nonverbal cue. Standing face to face with another person can be intimidating. A slight body angle or blade away from the person with whom you are conversing will present a much more accommodating nonverbal. It is also important how you shake hands. An open and friendly handshake is one that matches the confidence of the other person and also takes a palm up angle.

---

[4]Maurice Schweitzer, *Friend & Foe: When to Cooperate, When to Compete, and How to Succeed at Both*, Currency, 2015.

The Bandwagon Effect

The bandwagon effect causes people to adopt trends and ideas because others are adopting them (think stupid TikTok trends or more recently, the Korean craze after Squid Game). When we see other people—especially those we trust—vouching for something by wearing it, using it or talking it up, it colours our opinion of the object in question. Harness the power of the bandwagon effect and social proof by soliciting LinkedIn recommendations from current or former customers. Did you help a client achieve incredible results or earn a promotion? Ask them to write up a brief paragraph about your work together and share it for all to see on your profile page. Prospects coming to you cold might warm up to you a bit after reading a few glowing endorsements (especially if they know or share common connections with your referrer.)

Stroke Their Egos

Make him feel as if he were the only person in the room by listening as if he were the only person in the room. Examine him in the eyes. Show him you're paying attention by concentrating on what he's saying. It may seem obvious, but you'd be surprised how many people drift off, check their phones, let their eyes wander and so on. There is no faster way to demonstrate disinterest in someone. Please do not interrupt or finish her sentences. When she finishes saying something, wait a second before responding. This indicates you've really listened and you're taking it in.

Be 'Raw': Bring Up Your Own Bad Experiences

Try storytelling a mistake, sharing personal information, being silly with your staff and/or having one-on-one meetings to allow for a more naturally vulnerable conversation. When you plan the use and execution of storytelling, you'll reap the advantages it has in building trust.

This might seem counterintuitive—but digging up your target's negative emotions could pave the way for trust with you. By telling them your fake negative instances, you can make them feel they can tell you anything because you empathize. And once you know what they're insecure about and craving for, you already have loads of power.

Be a Copycat

This strategy is called mirroring and involves subtly mimicking another person's behaviour. Try to imitate someone's body language, gestures, and facial expressions when you're talking to them. When speaking to them, use their exact words. Please do not paraphrase. Instead, ask questions like, 'What kind of X are you (where X is one or more of their words)?' It's almost as if hearing their own words lulls their subconscious into trusting you.

Watch their gestures, noticing where they 'put' the things they are talking about in the space in and around themselves. Then, when you mention the same things, gesture to exactly the same place. As one delighted student puts it, 'It's as if you agree to treat their imaginary friends as real.' They'll soon believe that you see the world in exactly the same way as they do.

Say Their Name

Your name is an important part of your identity, and it feels great when others use it. Likeable people make a point of addressing others by name every time they see them. You should not only use someone's name when greeting him. According to research, when the person they're speaking with refers to them by name during a conversation, they feel validated. Equally important is remembering other details about their lives that they have shared with you previously—like the names of their partner, children, or if they have a pooch.

Find a Middle-Ground When You Talk to Them

Discovering areas of shared interest is an excellent way to deepen our level of connection with others and increase their appreciation of us. We connect and develop good relationships with those we have things in common with. The commonalities may not always be obvious; we may have to look for them. For example, I often had the opportunity to chat with a dedicated runner at the fitness facility that I work out at. Since I had no interest in running, there seemed to be no common grounds for a connection. However, most people like food, so I asked him what he ate before a major run. It gave us something in common to discuss.

Practise Your Act

If you're going to play the nice guy all the time, you'll need loads of practise. Stand in front of the mirror and practise what you're going to say; smile and nod empathetically. You are more likely to make something up on the spot if you are not well prepared. When you make something up on the spot, the other person is more likely to notice that you are lying or faking it.

- Consider audio and/or video recording yourself enacting an interaction at work. This will help you identify any awkward pauses or mannerisms that you do that may give you away.
- The more you can practise the better. If you rehearse a lot, it should feel very natural when you talk to the other person.

Do a Background Check

I already told you, people are *starved* for external validation. Mentally, they're looking to check a box indicating that they can form some sort of connection with you, however remote. That is why people engage in the name game. (I believe this has evolutionary roots dating back to when humanity was a collection of disparate tribes and people needed to validate who the stranger was and whether he was trustworthy.) Prior to sales calls, I conduct research on LinkedIn and social networks to identify any commonality, shared interests, or common connection. This is something I bring up early in the conversation. 'I see you went to school in...,' 'Oh my god, you know Mike as well?' and so on. Usually, it's a quick confirmation. 'Yes, Tom is a wonderful person. I went to the same school as him. 'How did you get to know him?' However, it goes a long way toward gaining their trust.

Tell Them *Your* Background

If you want them to get vulnerable, you have to trick them into believing you're getting vulnerable too.

In my opinion, the reason why people like Batman more than Superman is because Superman seems almost too unrealistic. He doesn't seem vulnerable enough for us to be emotionally invested. If you act like you're open and honest with how you speak to people, you'll exude strength but you'll also show vulnerability. You're not letting them know your weaknesses, you're just making them vomit all of their weaknesses out. It could be something like you cooking up a false story about how cruel your previous boss was or how you lost your (non-existent) pet cat a few days ago such that your target ends up doing things for you out of a sense of empathy. People trust vulnerability because it's believable and it shows that you are willing to put yourself out there. You have some skin in the game so people trust that you are invested in what you are saying.

Bridge the Gap, Temporarily

People are more likely to trust others who are at the same level as themselves. After meeting their patient, a psychologist may remove his or her lab coat. Schweitzer suggests that managers remove items from their offices that reinforce the fact that they have power over the other person in order to build trust among their employees. This could be as simple as taking off their suit jacket or tie, or it could mean holding the meeting in a different setting, such as going for a walk together or meeting in a coffee shop, which helps to break down the hierarchy rather than in an office where the boss is sitting behind a bigger desk in a bigger chair.

Make Them Ramble

Whether we want to admit it or not, we love to talk about ourselves. In fact, we love it so much that it produces the same pleasurable sensation in our brains as food and money. Harvard neuroscientists have even stated that it is so rewarding that we can't help but share our feelings. This makes sense when you consider that discussing our own beliefs and opinions, rather than those of others, stimulates the mesolimbic dopamine system, which is linked to the motivation and reward feelings we get from food, money and sex.

Everyone loves talking about themselves, especially when it's their own praise or something they're passionate about. When speaking to people, pay attention to what makes them become animated, lights up their face or sit up straight. These are opportunities for us to help the speaker get further into topics that are of great interest to them. This can help you form strong positive impressions and lasting memories.

The Power of an End-Point

I'm sure you've sat in a bar at some point and been approached by a stranger who tried to strike up a conversation. My guess is that you felt awkward, if not uncomfortable. This is because you had no idea when or if the conversation would come to an end. The first step in developing great rapport and having great conversations is to let the other person know that the end is in sight and it is very close. When you approach someone to start a conversation, most people first assess the situation for threat.

'I'm Rooting for You'

Most people long for someone to say, 'I get what you're saying,' 'You're absolutely right' or 'You deserve better.' This is especially true when a feeling of injustice or unfairness is involved. Charismatic people know that a little empathy goes a long way, however. Many people are satisfied just hearing 'I'm on your side' without seeing any behaviour to back up that claim. If someone swears over and over that they understand and support you, measure their actions against their words. If they don't match up, you might need to move on.

Five Takeaways for You to Skim Over:

- You can use people's desires, insecurities and need for belonging to get what you want.
- There is no person in this whole world who doesn't enjoy feeling validated or belonging.
- Your co-workers' and boss's trust in you is your biggest weapon.
- Gaining someone's trust by playing nice is an almost sure-shot way of peeking into their desires and weaknesses.
- Your tactics of persuasion work more on people who are either loners, narcissists or aggressors. You can have them in the palm of your hand in the workplace by influencing them.

3

A LITTLE LYING AT WORK (DOES NOBODY ANY HARM)

Lying is a cooperative act. Think about it. A lie has no power whatsoever by its mere utterance. Its power emerges when someone else agrees to believe the lie.[5]

—Pamela Meyer, American author,
certified fraud examiner, and entrepreneur.

Hey, don't scowl at the book. *Everyone* lies every now and again—and you will too. After all, lying helps us get what we want. But that happens only when others believe the lies you weave. So, you might as well do it right.

If I told you lying was good for you, you probably wouldn't believe me so easily. But trust me, I'm not lying. (See what I did there? But no, genuinely, I'm not lying.) Simply put, we lie because it works. When we do it well, we get what we want. We escape punishment, we sometimes get rewarded, we save ourselves from damage or embarrassment at work or we do it

---

[5]Pamela Meyer, 'How to spot a liar', TED, July 2011, https://www.ted.com/talks/pamela_meyer_how_to_spot_a_liar, Accessed on 8 February 2022.

just to always be the nice guy in the office.

We usually lie to maintain relationships and please others. And, of course, most people also lie to please ourselves and boost our confidence. We frequently tell lies to make ourselves appear and feel better, whether we're enhancing our credentials or strengthening our stories. Knowing how to get away with a few white lies can be a valuable skill. Giving your boss a nice little explanation for why you're late for work, for example, can be quite useful. Why do they need to know you hit the snooze button a few too many times?

From a young age, we're taught to believe that lying is a cardinal sin—one that can easily lose us friends, opportunities and instantly make us seem untrustworthy if we're found out. However, in spite of how often we're told that no good can come from lying, that's not always true. In some cases, the benefits of lying actually far outweigh those you'd get from telling the truth.

A few white lies around the office isn't the end of the world. In fact, they may even boost your productivity. Telling an overbearing boss that you're working on a project on his or her specific timeframe when, in fact, you're working on a timeframe that works better for you can help you placate power dynamics while allowing you to prioritize your own needs and abilities.

I know lying can be kind of scary because you're always at risk of being exposed. But don't worry too much. People are easily fooled. 'There is no Pinocchio's nose,' explains Paul Ekman, professor emeritus of psychology at the University of California. 'There's no sign that is always present when someone lies and always absent when someone is truthful.' 'Our default assumption is that people are telling the truth,' says Feldman.[6] And often, we don't actually want to hear the truth. If we hear what we want to hear, whether true or false, we accept it. Consider evaluating the work of a colleague. When we ask a friend if we did a good job, we want the answer to be 'yes,' regardless of its validity. We are unmotivated to investigate further once we hear it.

You know what? Let's go ahead and lie to ourselves a little: this isn't lying, it's called *tact*.

Step 1: Get your story straight. Figure out exactly what you're going to say. Prepare answers for any potential questions. Taking notes of your lie will help you remember it when it comes time to do the deed.

Step 2: Visualize your lie actually occurring. You won't be making things up as you go along; instead, you'll be remembering the event as if it actually happened.

Step 3: Keep eye contact. Liars avoid it unconsciously, which leads people to suspect something is wrong.

(Tip: Try not to smile too much. Liars have an unnatural smile.)

Step 4: Unwind! Fidgeting and sweating are tell-tale signs.

Step 5: Maintain control of your hands. Above all, keep them away from your face. According to studies, liars unconsciously touch their nose or mouth while lying.

---

[6]Lacey Rose, 'Lying Is Good For You', *Forbes*, 24 October 2005, https://www.forbes.com/2005/10/19/lying-dishonesty-psychology_cx_lr_comm05_1024lie.html?sh=34f63d5107c7, Accessed on 8 February 2022.

Step 6: Act unconcerned. Don't become defensive. Maintain a consistent tone of voice and refrain from protesting excessively. Act as if you don't care whether or not the person believes you. Fly away free and clear, like the liar bird that you are.

Step 7: Recognize when it's appropriate to stop talking. Another effective way to avoid being caught in a lie is to limit your chit-chat. Only say what you absolutely have to, lowering the chances that you'll say something suspicious or that your body language will reveal your true intentions.

- Stick to the story. Know what your story is down to the smallest details and don't veer away from it from one telling to the next.
- Lean in and try not to avoid someone's gaze.
- Breathe normally.
- Don't gulp or clear your throat excessively.

Bend Reality

Lying requires a lot more mental effort than telling the truth. Eliminate as much mental effort as possible by knowing the lie before telling it. Instead of making up an entire story, try to bend the truth. A person is much more likely to believe something that could actually happen. For example, instead of fabricating a story about attending a party, you could attend a party but lie about some of the details, such as who else attended and what you did. If you went out to eat with your family at a specific restaurant, you may lie and say you went to the restaurant with a date but tell the truth about what you ate.

Mix a Little Bit of Truth in There (So That You Sleep Well at Night Too)

If you're going to lie, keep as much of it as true as you can. 'Within your story, the foundation and many of the facts should be something that is true and something you know well,'[7] says Laura MacLeod, a therapist and HR expert and creator of *From the Inside Out Project*. She gives the example of you running late to meet your partner—perhaps because you've been shopping and spending more money than they would like. The story you tell your partner can include your trip to the store, your purchase of necessary items or your attempt to find necessary items, and maybe that the store was crowded so you had to wait in line—everything, except the overspending you did at the cash register.

'I'm a Terrible, Terrible Liar'

Pretend you're terrible at lying so when you really need to lie, people believe you're telling the truth. Fumble and murmur while telling some stupid white lies during casual conversations so that when you finally tell bigger lies (that get you what you want), without fumbling or getting jittery, people believe you're saying nothing but the truth.

---

[7] Alex Daniel, '17 Genius Ways to Lie Like a Spy', *yahoo!life*, 22 March 2019, https://www.yahoo.com/lifestyle/15-genius-ways-lie-spy-185849407.html, Accessed on 8 February 2022.

Keep it Short and Sweet

When you lie, there is a tendency to add a lot of extra information and details that you usually would not. The other person may wonder why you are talking so much. Also, you may start to provide details that do not make sense.

For example, it is preferable to say, 'I woke up late this morning,' rather than, 'I drank coffee last night to stay up and work on this project, and then I couldn't fall asleep. I finally fell asleep, and it was a struggle to get out of bed this morning.' Only respond to a question posed by another individual.

Lastly, *Know* Your Target

Good liars have the same gift as good communicators: the ability to get inside the listener's head. Empathy not only helps you understand what your listener wants to hear, but it also helps you avoid tripping over tripwires that will raise their suspicions. 'To make a credible lie, you need to take into account the perspective of your target,' says Carolyn Saarni, co-editor of the book *Lying and Deception in Everyday Life*. 'Know what they know. Be aware of their interests and activities so you can cover your tracks.'[8]

Speaking of targets, here are some things to consider *before* you start working that mind magic.

A Group Mentality

If you're a member of a group, then you're statistically less likely to be convinced of subjects or ideas that go against the views

---

[8] Carolyn Saarni, *Lying and Deception in Everyday Life*, Guilford Press, 1993.

of your fellow group members. The existence of the group and your loyalty to it tend to strengthen your resolve to stick with their version of the truth—even if it's completely inaccurate.

The Loners

Those who consider themselves socially inadequate tend to be more easily persuaded. Even if they're no more socially inept than others, the fact that they see themselves that way leads them to place the burden of conversation on the person they're interacting with. This makes it easier for that person to persuade them without challenge.

The Narcissists

These are people who believe or want to believe they're special and destined for greatness. They're more likely to believe impossibly good things can—and should—happen to them to feed their egos, and thereby, their soul. Make them feel they're your greatest asset in the office and they will do anything for you. Anything.

The Ones with Dark Thoughts

Research shows that people who are depressed are more easily convinced to accept someone else's views over their own. This tendency is largely due to factors like lack of aggression and self-esteem, as mentioned above. However, you may find that some people who experience depression are not actually persuaded by you but simply agree with you to avoid conflict—which is good enough for you to have your way at work. Just remember, you're not being malicious; you're only persuading them.

The Aggressors

If you don't like to show aggression, then you're more likely to be overtaken by a smooth talker who is fluent in the art of persuasion. Even if they make you feel uneasy about whatever they're trying to persuade you of, a lack of aggressiveness makes it easier for someone to sway your beliefs. People who are not prone to displaying violence usually do not challenge what others are saying. Look out for the aggressive ones—they're your main enemies in the workplace. Whatever happens, you *cannot* stoop down to their level. That blows your cover, after all.

The Ones Low on Self-Esteem

People with low self-esteem are statistically far easier to convince than those with higher self-esteem. This is most likely because those with low self-esteem tend to value others' opinions more than their own. The biggest challenge you'll have to face here is determining the self-esteem level of the person you're trying to persuade. You can do this by analysing factors such as body posture, confidence of tone and commitment to their point of view.

Five Takeaways for You to Skim Over:

- Lying at work isn't the problem, lying and getting caught red-handed is.
- A few white lies here and there are essential for you to keep up your nice guy persona. Sometimes, it's easier to make things up than to risk disappointing people, especially when those people are the ones giving you what you want.

- You have to lie to others at work to make them feel good. You know that, mostly, being kind is better than being completely honest, especially when you want to expand your corporate network.
- A few white lies are also motivational tools. You can't tell your boss he's an idiot and that you know better than him. You have to lie to him and make him feel like a genius. Lying also helps you avoid confrontation—getting the person doing the confronting calmed down, confused or charmed.
- Lying about a better offer or saying you're ready to walk out the door when you're not getting your way can help you get what you want and is pretty much expected of you, anyway.

4

YOU HAVE TO BE THE NICEST ONE IN THE OFFICE

It's not that you aren't likable. On the contrary. You are. It's just that one wonders if you haven't made a career out of being so likable.[9]

—Jerzy Kosinski, Polish-American author.

Have you noticed there are people who always seem to be more likable? And have you also noticed they're the ones who get everything they want, without much opposition or effort? Think of Barack Obama: he was *extremely* likable. He seemed to be a great father and family man, he had a good sense of humour, and he liked things that the common person related to, be it basketball, football, or popstar concerts. It didn't matter if people didn't agree with his opinions, they were still swayed by him. Or, think about the teacher's pet in class: they'd say the homework should be cancelled and voila, it would be cancelled. How? Because they knew what the teacher wanted to hear; they knew how to be the most likeable person in the classroom. The office is no

---

[9] Jerzy Kosinski, *Blind Date*, Grove Press, 1998.

different. As James Fallon said, 'You don't manipulate by snarling, you manipulate by being sweet as shit!' Smart mind-masters at work make their peers feel *great* to maximize their output but then maximize selfish self-interest by only manoeuvring for their own promotions. Kind of dark, but true.

There's always that person in your life you admire (or, let's be honest, envy) from afar: the funny—but intelligent—co-worker, the admirable boss with a kick-ass routine or even that friend of yours who can get just about anyone in your office to smile (even on a bad day).

Here's a big secret you've probably never told yourself: that could be you as well. Seriously, being liked by people does not include performing a magic or conjuring up a grand illusion. Gaining respect at work, having a lot of friends, or performing as a strong leader isn't reserved for a select few. It's a talent that just about anyone can learn—and learn quickly.

In a recent episode of the new ABC drama *Mind Games*, One of the characters notes an intriguing personality feature that distinguishes the most popular people: they admit their flaws more quickly than they wait for them to be disclosed over time. The show is about using cunning tricks to manipulate others and ensure a positive outcome and so, it's a bit ridiculous but there's truth in the observation.

Let me tell you an interesting story: two politicians in England were running for Prime Minster. Both men wanted to 'win' the position of becoming England's next Prime Minster. It was planned for one woman to eat dinner with each of them on two consecutive nights. 'When I left the dining table after sitting next to Gladstone, I believed he was the cleverest man in England,' she said of each of them. 'But after sitting next to Disraeli, I felt like the smartest lady there.'

You're aware of what occurred next, aren't you? That year, Disraeli won the election and became the next Prime Minister!

Candidates who are disliked frequently lose elections to those who are liked (charismatic). Think about it for yourself? Who would you want to pick as the winner: a person you like or a person you don't really care for? I imagine you'll go with the person you like. The same is true for anything that requires picking people. Most people pick the person they like over the person who they detest. What was Disraeli's secret sauce to winning the election? It's simple: Disraeli was more likeable. He made people around him feel important, valued and even 'clever' when they were with him. Whereas, Gladstone did not pay attention towards other people. Gladstone was more focused on himself and his own accomplishments.

It isn't looks. It isn't education. It's not even superior knowledge or talent. Put simply, it's likability. And it is simple (when we think about it). In the long term, likable people win out over all others. They are more enjoyable to work with, instil loyalty in their peers, and are 'lighter to lift' inside any team or company. At some point in our lives, it is clear that we have the necessary skills, talent, and capacities to execute our jobs. What keeps a lot of individuals from progressing to the next level is how other people perceive us. Managers and executives desire likeable employees on their teams while making hiring decisions and planning their career growth. We are all human beings before we are professionals. It is natural to desire to be around people who are upbeat. If two persons are equally capable of doing a task, selling a product or service (or even sitting next to us), the person who is more liked will always win.

Unlikeable people, often unintentionally, become unpleasant to others and detrimental to their own job advancement. They lose terrific employees if they are managers. The unfortunate aspect is that a lack of self-awareness is largely to blame.

Charm gets you places. It is a magical quality that makes people like you. When you have charm, you can basically get what you want. It will open doors for you and bring promotions to you. It will even get you that big project you would love to manage. What is charm and how do you get it? Is it about being good-looking, having an extraordinary personality or your uncle's infectious laugh? Or maybe, it's a blend of how you present yourself along with your knowledge of others?

People who are charming have the ability to attract and engage others. They are frequently accepted into inner circles because they present themselves well, speak well, and act debonairly. When it comes to achieving success in life, don't rely on the 'X factor.' Instead, consider your 'L factor.' Are you appealing? Are you certain? It may influence whether you receive raises, promotions, or invites. In some circumstances, it may even surpass competence and skill. It's not an easy task. It takes practise, but it is doable. When firms decide who to hire, the 'L factor' plays a significant role. It all comes down to that elusive fit: most applicants are talented, but it's much more difficult to find someone who is easy to get along with.

Can you make yourself more likable? 'Absolutely,' experts say, including myself.

Why Are Likeable People So Magnetic?

1. **No** (or minimal) **ego** (seemingly, they're basically great at acting like they're selfless.) Who likes an ego? No one.
2. **People with likeable characteristics are more likely to get help, support, care and things they want from others.**

Think about it for yourself. How likely are you to reach out and help someone who has been helpful, kind and just amazing towards you? You might feel an inkling to help that person out.

3. **Likeable people are relatable.** Likable people 'are similar to us in terms of origin, personality, or interests,' which makes us believe their interests include ours or will help us achieve ours. Great speakers use this technique to connect with their audience. I met a high-profile attorney who shares many personal stories in his public speeches but he almost always starts with a story about his grandmother. 'Everyone has a grandma,' he told me; It's an instant connection!

4. **Likable people elevate others.** They praise, share credit and enjoy other people's successes. Funnily enough, this quality elevates them the most. It's a testament to the lovely old truth that we keep what we give away.

5. **They're great at pretending to be all for others**. They're seemingly humble. Think of Kanye West—he's extremely prosperous, but also extremely obnoxious. Consider Barack Obama: he is both tremendously successful and incredibly humble. Whether you like or dislike Kanye West's music, there's no disputing his absolute confidence and arrogance. Whether you agree or disagree with Obama's views, you can't ignore his extraordinary confidence and humility. There is a fine line and people—who are enjoyable to be around—avoid egocentric, self-centred and bragging individuals.

6. **Have an appropriate sense of humour.** Think about it. When was the last time someone you just met cracked a joke and you thought, wow I hate this guy/girl? Probably never. It seems obvious but people who are enjoyable to be around genuinely have a great sense of humour.

7. **They also ask lots of questions, drawing out their colleagues and superiors.** After asking questions, likeable people listen closely to the replies, giving the other person their entire attention and frequently asking follow-up questions for clarification. And, of course, charming people never interrupt the person with whom they are conversing—the kiss of death for being perceived as likeable. Remember, people *love* talking about themselves and the mind-game master plays it to his advantage.
8. **They make us feel relaxed.** Less-likable people create stress, tension and can even make people defensive and on-edge. Those emotions are not enjoyable.
9. **'All else being equal, people do business with people they like,'** says Jeffrey Gitomer, author of *The Little Red Book of Selling*.[10] This isn't limited to salespeople. It applies to all connections, both internal and societal. To constantly achieve what you want, you must present yourself as the pleasant guy.
10. **Negativity repels.** This is a simple concept that is frequently misunderstood. Even if it is not intended at us, a negative attitude makes us want to avoid the person who is causing it. Positivity, on the other hand, is quite appealing. People with dislikeable characteristics are more likely to be rejected, neglected and abandoned. Consider it for yourself. How likely are you to assist someone who has been nasty and disrespectful to you? It would be difficult to accomplish.

If you want to be more charismatic, consider the following riddle: what makes you attractive even if you're not attractive?

---

[10] Jeffrey Gitomer, *The Little Red Book of Selling*, Bard Press, 2004.

What draws people's attention even if you're impoverished? What invisible 'magic' can captivate, persuade, inspire and hypnotize others? You're ahead of me because, of course, you have charisma. Like gravity, which cannot be seen but has powerful effects, we can't 'see' charisma but we know when someone has it. Charmers are:

- Considered 'strangely attractive' (even if their looks aren't great).
- Able to lead others naturally in thought and action.
- Able to influence and persuade others.
- Able to get their way without causing rifts or drama.
- Popular amongst everyone at work.
- Able to make an impression on first meetings and be remembered.
- Able to make other people feel happier or sadder just by being close to them.

Here are some sure-shot ways to become the *nicest* person at work and charm them all out of their wits:

Show Up on Time, *Always*

You don't have to be the queen of social graces to charm the pants off everyone and punctuality is a great example of that. By simply showing up on time, you'll get huge brownie points while also proving to your host (or interviewer, or future boss) that you're one heck of a reliable person. 'It shows you value their time,' said Jennifer Cohen on Forbes.[11] And people prefer that.

---

[11]Jennifer Cohen, '7 Ways To Charm The Pants Off Of Everyone,

Do a Little Background Check

Research your employees, your boss, your new customers and clients. Search through LinkedIn, Google and Facebook to find out all you can about them, especially something you have in common with them that could be a conversation starter. Where did they live? What businesses have they worked for? What have they accomplished? What people do you have in common? What are their accomplishments? What are their interests? Charming people understand that nothing is more flattering than when someone takes the effort to get to know them. They are quick to notice that you have something in common with them. They remain completely focused on you.

Know What's Up

There's nothing most painful than watching someone fake their way through a conversation. This happens with all sorts of topics—sports, movies, books—but never more so than with the news. So, save yourself the agony and show up to events having read the news. 'It'll prove to be a great conversation starter and shows you care about what's happening in the world around you,'[12] Cohen said. And there's nothing more charming than that.

All The Time', Forbes, 20 August 2014, https://www.forbes.com/sites/jennifercohen/2014/08/20/7-ways-to-charm-the-pants-off-of-everyone-all-the-time/?sh=1a5083761aba, Accessed on 8 February 2022.
[12]Ibid.

Play the Name-Game

If forgetting names is an issue that you deal with often, it may be time to play the name game. For starters, it's entirely understandable that, upon meeting a crowd of five or more people, your brain begins to shut down after the second person has introduced themselves. When you're first being introduced to someone, repeat their name back to him or her to emphasize that at least you care enough to remember them. Aside from that, simple tricks using random rhyming and alliteration can help you remember your peer Nero (example) as: 'Nero the Hero!' It's kind of childish but Nero will appreciate it when you remember his name at the brainstorm session.

Show Up Every Now and Then

Humans like things that are familiar, so just seeing you around in person makes you more likable to others. 'This concept gives a whole new meaning to the idea of face time,' Tiziana Casciaro, Professor of Organizational Behaviour, suggests. 'When you have the opportunity to relate to your colleagues face-to-face, do so. Swing by a co-worker's desk rather than messaging him. Go to after-work drinks if you have time and would find the outing enjoyable—if not, just try to talk to people as much as possible in person during work hours,' she advised.[13] You want to maximize rich interactions and cut down on the drier ones

---

[13] Tiziana Cascario, 'Competent Jerks, Lovable Fools, and the Formation of Social Networks', *Harvard Business Review*, June 2005, https://hbr.org/2005/06/competent-jerks-lovable-fools-and-the-formation-of-social-networks, Accessed on 8 February 2022.

like texts and phone calls. Be sure to be seen.

Make Them Feel Like Pop-Stars

When you meet someone famous, how would you greet him or her? You'd probably look him or her in the eyes, smile adoringly, shake hands warmly, be forceful but caring, be on your toes projecting confidence, and remark how nice it is to meet him or her. Charming folks have a kind demeanour. They greet you as though you are the most amazing person and that it is such an honour to finally meet you. They transport you to the red carpet at the Academy Awards.

Make Them Laugh a Little

It's hard to hate a jokester or someone who has a carefree approach to life. Usually, the most-liked people are those who can fill a room with laughter. It's understandable if it's not in your nature to laugh. Just make sure you're prepared to notice the humour in anything. Be someone who can readily laugh and smile. You'll win them over.

Tell Them Your Shortcomings

Trust me, this works like magic. Tell them what you lack (even if it's fake) and they'll tell you all their insecurities and hollow-points. Once you find their hollow-points, you know what language to speak to convince them to do almost anything. You basically make them see what *you* want them to see—they never get a glimpse into your real weaknesses and that, right there, is subtle power-play at work.

That character on the show *Mind Games* is right: Admitting your flaws makes you more likeable. People usually find them out on their own. Of course, you should avoid acting like a victim and sharing your issues with everyone you encounter. It's acceptable to start a meeting by discussing the difficulties you're facing at work. People are more likely to suggest a few solutions, come to your aid and even pat you on the back. They're also willing to do almost anything to help you out because they're blinded by your 'authenticity'; I speak from sheer experience.

It's All About Them, Not You

Nope, not in reality. In reality, you're merely making it seem like it's all about them, so *you* can get what you want. But yes, you have to make them feel you're all about them. When you're having conversations with others, make sure that the focus is not only on you, your problems, your life or your opinions. In fact, approach conversations with the intent that it's not an opportunity for you to unload your every grievance on another person but perhaps a chance for you to get to know someone better, to learn something from them or to connect in a way you haven't before.

Ask for Suggestions and They'll Give You Their Entire Trust

When you ask others for their expertise, wisdom or guidance, you're not only potentially receiving great advice for yourself, you're also tapping into their strengths, which makes anyone feel good.

Put That Smartphone Away

People are all about themselves and so they hate when you don't listen to them rambling about their new achievement or how well their son has done in math class. To charm, you have to be present! 'Nothing will turn someone off to you like a mid-conversation text message or even a quick glance at your phone,' says Dr Travis Bradberry, who introduced The Emotional Intelligence Appraisal. 'You will find that conversations are more…effective when you immerse yourself in them.' [14]

Don't Claim to Know Everything

We all know how important it is to steer clear of the office know-it-all. Why is that? Part of the reason is—we know that person won't ask for our help and we like to be helpful. More importantly, those who have all of the answers are usually pushing their own agenda. In their conceited attitude, they exhibit a sense of pride that's not attractive to anyone.

Why So Serious?

I'll admit that I'm having trouble with this one. I'm a serious individual with serious problems (most of the time). However, in life, it is preferable to look at the big picture. People who are very serious are inherently selfish since they are preoccupied with their personal problems. People who are highly pleasant at work are those who can lay aside their issues and go with

---

[14] Travis Bradberry, *The Emotional Intelligence Quick Book*, Simon and Schuster, 2005.

the flow. They're selfless.

Instead of 'Okay, But', Use 'I See What You're Saying, and...'

If you find yourself caught in a challenging conversation about a sensitive topic, use the 'and not but' rule. Instead of invalidating or cancelling out what someone is saying, show that you honour their opinion by shifting your language to suggest that you understand where they are coming from and would like to offer even more to possibly consider. They could be talking absolute nonsense, but you cannot make that evident on your face or through your language. Remember, the diplomatic warrior wins in the long-run.

The Teeny-Tiny Observations Matter

Awkward silences: meet your new enemy—practicing positive observation. There's nothing worse than sitting in an uncomfortable silence with someone while quickly scanning through all forms of small talk in your head deciding which is the least painful. Instead of idle chitchat, learn from other charming folks by picking out one positive observation about the person you're trying to speak with. Pay attention to your surroundings, including the people in them, and utilize them to your advantage in winning over everyone in the room. Look around and try to make new acquaintances. Take note of who is around you and what interests or attracts you about them. Find something unique about what they're wearing and commend it. The important thing to remember here is that a generic comment like 'Nice dress!' isn't enough. It should be considerably more precise, and it should usually be followed with a question. 'What a fascinating watch!' you could say, for example. 'From where did you get it?' Alternatively, you may remark something like, 'Wow, that purple makeup looks amazing!' 'Do you match your makeup to your clothing all the time?' Saying 'I love your shoes. Can you tell me where you got them?' goes a lot further than 'So this weather we're having...'

The Look-Upgrade

While you don't have to be Megan Fox or Tom Cruise, looking the best version of yourself plays a major role in how charming you are—be it at work or beyond it. The way you dress each day communicates a message. If you take the time to present yourself in a sharp way, with a careful attention to detail, others will perceive you as a conscientious and enigmatic presence. On the other hand, if you're a sloppy, unassuming dresser, this communicates to others that you have low self-esteem and would rather fade into the background. Command the room by dressing sharply and soon, others will buy into your charms.

Your Body Talks More Than Your Mouth Does

As we know, 70 per cent of our communication is non-verbal. Body language plays a very important role in the perception of people. It's important to use the right body language to be trusted and be liked by others. Ensure your arms and legs are not crossed. Use gestures while talking because hands symbolize trust. Point your feet and torso towards the person talking, as it shows you are interested in the person you are talking to. These are powerful non-verbal techniques that help in building rapport. Also, whenever you do talk, avoid shouting or coming across as aggressive. Always use a relaxed and gentle tone of voice.

Create Images: Hypnotize

Charismatic people inspire emotion and feeling in other people. It is critical to utilize language correctly. Don't merely say things to convey information and facts; instead, utilize them to create experiences in the minds of your listeners. This quickly increases your charisma.

'I boarded a ship. There was a storm,' says the narrator, but consider this: 'The ship was enormous, completely black. We could feel the waves fiercely rolling as we moved forward, making it impossible to walk on deck. I could taste salt on my lips and felt saltwater spray on my face. And you should have heard the screaming all around!' Charismatics involve you; they create an atmosphere, tension, and excitement through their descriptive power. Don't just tell me what happened; help me experience it by telling me the sounds, smells, tastes, sights, feelings and textures involved in the experience.

Let Them in on a Little Secret

This secret could even be made up. Who gets to know except for you? Our human race is built on the concept of gossips, stories and secrets. Self-disclosure is one of the best relationship-building techniques. Sharing secrets gets people together. People feel in command and worthy when someone tells them a secret because you need to earn a reputation. This makes people instantly feel good about themselves. If you make someone feel good, they will immediately take a liking towards you. Share something about yourself with the group that they may not know. This will help in building rapport. Begin with something like, 'I don't usually disclose this, however, I feel you'll understand…'

Get a Little Hands-On

Touch can influence behaviour, increase the chances of compliance, make the person making the contact seem more attractive and friendly and can even help you make a sale.

Say you're congratulating someone; shaking hands or (possibly better yet, depending on the situation) patting them gently on the shoulder or upper arm can help reinforce the sincerity of your words.

Be a Master Story-Teller

You all know that one friend who lights up a room with the retelling of a simple story, making every moment come to life and keeping you hanging on the edge of your seat with laughter and suspense. Good storytelling is a fine art—and a nearly extinct one at that. Building your confidence and speaking abilities will assist with this, but taking an improv class is another wonderful method to tell more lively stories. It will force you out of your comfort zone and get you used to thinking on the go and creating stories.

Lose to Win

Huh? What does *that* mean? It means a charmer makes it clear they're not afraid to lose—they cannot be seen as a threat by anyone else and so, they pretend they do not want to win. In reality, you could be a sore loser; however, don't show it at work, ever. Charming people don't try to win at everything openly. On the contrary, their aim is to show they are willing to give more without expecting anything in return. For them, it's not difficult to admit their mistakes, failures or talk about their weaknesses because they want to win not just one battle but the overall workplace war. And it's something that not everyone can do. They can openly say, 'I'm jealous of you,' or 'I can't do this, please teach me,' because they know people appreciate honesty and real emotion. They basically know how to stroke egos well while making it seem like they don't have any themselves.

Charmers Are Silly, They're Human

Maybe ice skating or Twister is not their strong point but they're absolutely not afraid to be awkward. Curiously enough, people respect them even more because of this. When you're ready to demonstrate your weaknesses and you're not afraid to look silly, people don't laugh at you. They laugh with you. Because everybody understands that all of this is fine.

Pass the Waiter-Test

If you want everyone to know you're the nicest, show you're nice not just to them but to everyone. It seems incredibly basic but, believe it or not, it needs to be said: have good manners. You don't necessarily need to know which fork is for the salad and which is for the shrimp—but simple things like saying 'please' and 'thank you' and excusing yourself, when necessary, during an office lunch or a dinner with a client can go a long, *long* way. Using manners shows that you're considerate of others which makes people want to be around you. Also, in an interesting article published in *Psychology Today*, professor Paul J. Zak explains, 'When someone is nice towards another person, the recipient's brain releases oxytocin and this causes him or her to respond with kindness.'[15]

I don't know about you, but it truly amazes me how some small behaviours can trigger chemical reactions in someone else's brain.

Be Confident But Approachable; Always

Body language speaks volumes about who you are. Charming people glide into a room with confidence, but they don't necessarily take the whole spotlight. A leader may want to take the strongest stance they can muster, but a charmer wants to stay approachable and likeable. After all, making others feel valued is part of what charisma is all about. Turn your knees or face toward them when someone speaks to you so they know you're interested.

Do Not Complain; A Complete No-No

Niceness is all about positivity, even if it is performed. You might be envious of what someone else has or you might be sour over not getting a particular project to lead, but do not show it. Act like you accept it with grace. Try to be optimistic. Keep your glass half-full. Be enthusiastic. Don't trot out all your issues. No one wants to be with a Debbie Downer. We all have

---

[15] Paul J. Zak, 'Why Manners Matter…even to the French', *Psychology Today*, 28 July 2012, https://www.psychologytoday.com/us/blog/the-moral-molecule/201207/why-manners-matter, Accessed on 8 February 2022.

problems, but compartmentalize them, park them in a corner and bring them out for close friends and family.

Say It Like You Mean It (Even If You Don't)

Well, makes sense, doesn't it? If charismatic people express more through their movement, expressions, voice and eyes, then learning to be more expressive will instantly make you more charismatic. Remember: charisma amounts to emotional infectiousness. Use the 43 muscles in your face to smile more. Start taking acting classes and practising projecting your voice. Learn to appreciate language and mould words so that when you talk, people pay attention. Infuse your communication with vitality. Examine how charismatic people captivate others by expressing energy through their face and eyes, as well as how they speak and what they say.

Maintain Some Mystery; Leave Them Wanting More

When we say that someone has 'a certain something,' ever noticed how that something can never really be described? I don't want you to keep everything about yourself hidden or act like you're a spy, but silence may be powerful. You don't always have to be the one shouting the loudest or expressing your opinions on everything. On occasion, silence possesses both power and dignity. You're not 'trying to be charming' by keeping a little mystery about yourself; all you're doing is holding back a little (in a culture where we're all pushed to divulge everything about ourselves to everyone, even on national television). It's possible that chasing attention, shouting louder than the next person, and telling every stranger your life story will get you somewhere, but it won't make you charismatic.

Five Takeaways for You to Skim Over:

- Nice guys *don't* ever finish last in the office. In fact, they're the first ones to get what they want without openly pissing anyone off.
- Master mind-controllers don't rule by yelling or banging fists but rather by creating a cult of personality with their charm and charisma.
- If you play nice guy, nobody ever suspects you of being a selfish person. You have your way always and also make them feel like they're having theirs.
- Nice guys know who to make everything about the other person to have their way—they listen more than they talk; they validate the other person to charm them.
- Nice guys never complain, whine, gossip (openly) or yell. They are bright sources of sunshine who pulls everyone in.

5

MAGNETIC MYSTERY

An elusive, enigmatic aura will make people want to know more, drawing them into your circle... The moment people feel they know what to expect from you, your spell on them is broken.[16]

—Robert Greene, author of *The Art of Seduction* and *The 48 Laws of Power*.

People like people who like them. This is one of social psychology's most often replicated discoveries. Those, on the other hand, like people who might like them. This is one of the most well-known seduction principles. A person is temporarily happy when they receive clear signals of interest from another person, adapts fast, and the case is closed. When a person's interest is shaky, though, they can't think of anything else; they're always looking for an explanation. Finally, the person interprets these thoughts as a sign of liking and thinks to themselves, 'Gee, I must really like this person since I can't stop thinking about him!' Every petal pulled off the rose while saying, 'He

---

[16]Robert Greene, *The Art of Seduction*, Penguin Books, 2003.

loves me, he doesn't love me...' is a step closer to attraction. And yes, this isn't just applicable to the world of romance, this is applicable to the corporate world too.

Think of James Bond for a moment. Quiet, pensive, confident and mysterious. Do you believe he was an extrovert or an introvert? Of course, I'm an introvert. Bond would have a lot of difficulties attracting ladies if he followed today's typical pick-up advice. What do you think? Making jokes, putting on a loud and boisterous show, and positioning himself as the party's life. Doesn't it feel a little off? That's because it's not the one. Bond, on the other hand, is *enigmatic*, a *badass*, *intriguing* and quietly *confident*. That combination is irresistible to women everywhere apparently and even to your co-workers and superiors.

Is it necessary to be James Bond to possess the same type of charisma? Not in the least. You can focus solely on bettering yourself in a way that feels good to you as long as you're an introvert, and your nature will take care of the rest. Charm, persuasion and the ability to create illusions are just a few of the seducer's many brilliant gifts—the captivating figure who can manipulate, deceive, and provide pleasure all at the same time. It could even make you more attractive in *anyone's* eyes. The compulsive need to reveal too much information about yourself and your feelings must be repressed, *especially at work*.

Uncertainty makes people wonder. It causes you to think about someone more. You may feel wonderful when you know someone likes you and you know everything there is to know about them, but that feeling is often short. When you get a feeling that someone likes you but aren't sure whether you think about them more, you're actually hooked. Consider the following scenario: you're seated in a pub with two equally gorgeous people. One brings you a drink and approaches you to talk. The other smiles and establishes a slight eye contact with you. Things are simple with the one who expressed their views up front, but you keep gazing towards the other person because you're not sure what's going on. That is what makes being mysterious so appealing. Playing hard to get or being unavailable isn't what mystery is about. It's all about not giving too much away when it comes to mystery. In the office, mystery entails being present but not overly so. When you're too available, people downplay your power and take you for granted—you only create value at work through selective absence.

Mysterious people are attractive because humans are naturally curious and want to know more about them. When you allow people's imaginations to fill in the gaps about you, they'll be drawn in to see if their assumptions prove to be correct. As Bede Jarrett, historian and author, rightly said, 'The mysterious is always attractive. People will always follow a vail.'[17]

Whether you want to appear a little more intriguing than you really are, seem a bit more exciting than your actual self is or you want to make someone realize how valuable you are by creating the impression that you actually have options and there are lots of things going on for you, this bag of tricks will prove to be useful.

---

[17]Bede Jarrett, 'The vocation to marriage eighteen discourses', Sheed & Ward, 1935.

What Makes a Mysterious Person So Magnetic?

- These people don't talk about what they have done or what things have happened in their day. This is the reason why you get more curious about knowing them more.
- Reading their minds is practically difficult, and it certainly draws you in. You feel compelled to study their thoughts and learn more about them.
- These people develop close relationships with very few people, and this tempts you to be one of them.
- You might sense that they are very sensitive and emotional people deep down due to which you want them to open up to you.
- They can construct a barrier between the outside world and themselves, making them appear self-sufficient and thus more appealing.
- They are unconcerned about what is going on around them because their own world is far superior to the real one.
- They will not be interested in you if you are really social and attractive. This will irritate you much and eventually cause you to obsess over them.
- You may feel compelled to grab their arms, shake them, and shout for them to see you, but they will stay uninterested despite your efforts.
- These individuals are smarter and like to spend more time alone, observing and questioning.
- They are unconcerned with what other people do or say around them; thus, they never gossip.
- They're quite relaxed. They offer sound advice that is worth considering, and they never make rash decisions.

- They have outstanding observation skills. They'll be able to deduce what you're attempting to express from the actions or words you use.
- Even though you will be together with such a person, you can never be the centre of their lives. They are more passionate about the hobbies that they possess.
- They do not get angry very easily. They are very good at controlling their anger and keeping it to themselves.
- Their views and ideas are never ordinary. You will be able to explore new points of view from every angle they have presented.
- They are calm and charismatic, yet they do not perform any specific actions to impress others.
- You'll never be able to fully comprehend the intriguing people, which means you'll never be bored and your love will never end.

Why Do Peers Who Are Too Available Lose Power at Work?

I'm a good employee. I'm on time. I work late. I'm there when my manager needs me. I'm reliable. So, why is someone else getting the promotion? Are you *too* reliable? Bosses *love* reliable employees (because they're easy to take advantage of—let's be honest here). Clients and customers seek out dependability. Friends and family know who to call in a pinch. How, then, can being reliable be bad? It's an awesome trait and more people should be skilled in this art. At work, however, the scales can tip. You can become too reliable. Nothing can make you feel more inferior than when you think someone is taking advantage of you. Feeling that your value is overlooked or that your boss doesn't notice your contributions should signal career danger. You can only win in subtle and sneaky power-play if you're not too available all the time.

You lose power by being a pushover

Nobody respects a pushover. It's normal to want to please your boss or co-workers but there are people who will take advantage of your good nature. Not everyone's performance is the same. Sometimes there's dead weight—people who don't contribute as much as they should. If the work needs to get done, someone must pick up that slack. Because you are the reliable one, you end up doing work that someone else should be doing. While it's great to pitch in, there is a limit to how much you can do without feeling annoyed.

Your time isn't valued

There are certain positions in which you need to be available in times of emergency. Sometimes, however, work can wait. True story: I once had a boss who would send emails at off-hours throughout the weekend and then chastise his staff on Monday morning if he did not get an immediate response. There were no emergencies. It was simply the power of wanting to control every aspect of his employees' personal time. There's no circumstance where that is acceptable. You have a right to privacy out of the office.

You're always getting your hands dirty

If most of your job duties continually fall below your level of expertise, you may be taken advantage of if it is because nobody else wants to do it. If you are constantly performing at a lower level, it makes it harder for you to stay relevant in your field. Boredom will creep in and you won't feel challenged.

You get taken advantage of

Are you regularly working extra hours, are you constantly feeling burnt out or are you your employer's go-to person for anything and everything? You need to take a step back and think: are you being asked to do something because of your skills, or is your employer taking advantage of your good nature?

While it's important to be a team player, you can only squeeze in so much work in a day. If you notice that your boss or co-worker is constantly adding tasks to your plate, you are the only person who will stand up for yourself.

You're never appreciated

Your boss can appreciate what you offer but they don't always tell you. Some managers are simply not good with providing positive feedback or praise. If work is repeatedly being piled-up and you never hear praise, something is out of balance. You'll never be thanked for all that you do but seeing respect for your hard work is necessary if you want to feel like a valuable part of the team.

You lose all your confidence

Your productivity is low, you're bitter and you're not noticed by anyone at work because you're *always* there. What does this lead to? This leads to a loss of power; a loss of confidence and that, my friend, is a bullet right into the heart or brain of a charmer who always gets his/her way.

Let me tell you a story: in college, I was always the first to raise my hand in class (a behaviour that earned me few friends, to say the least). As a freelance writer, I'm no stranger to that same over-eagerness when it comes to work, which manifests itself in quick responses and more than a few emojis. Being friendly and approachable was kind of my thing: emails, tweets, slack messages—you name it—until I learned the power of being absent at times. While common wisdom suggests that we should seize every chance that comes our way, there are some benefits to playing hard to get. Numerous studies have shown that opportunities are seen to be more valuable as they become less available—meaning that people want more of what they can't have, according to Robert Cialdini, a leading expert on influence and the author of *Pre-Suasion: A Revolutionary Way to Influence and Persuade.* 'What the scarcity principle says is that people are more attracted to those options or opportunities that are rare, unique or dwindling in availability,'[18] Dr Cialdini said. The reason behind this idea has to do with the psychology of 'reactance'. Essentially, when we think something is limited to us, we tend to want it more. Mystery is always alluring, and so, while you have to be likeable, you cannot make this charm available too often—you have to make your peers and bosses crave for it by remaining at a one-arm-distance.

And of course, the more mysterious you are, the lesser you can be manipulated—why? Because you never let people know your *actual* weak points. Quite logical, right?

How Do You Surround Yourself with Some Magnetic Mystery?

- **Be a stoic:** Animated people don't leave much to the imagination because they are the centre of attention. Appear quiet, somewhat serious, and reasonably even-keeled to be

---

[18] Robert Cialdini, *Pre-Suasion: A Revolutionary Way to Influence and Persuade*, Random House 2016.

appearing mysterious. No matter how frantic things are around you, be the calm in the middle of the storm. This isn't to imply you're devoid of emotion or passion; rather, you choose not to debase yourself by appearing too emotional, reactive, or ridiculously exuberant. Rather, choose to accept life as it is. React calmly to any news that comes your way and approach everything with a 'well, when I look into it, I'll make up my mind' attitude. Overreacting, acting childishly, bouncing with joy or fainting with worry are not behaviours you engage in. Enigmatic people never reveal much about themselves, which is why they make excellent natural leaders.

- **Know when to leave:** Yes, the last ones to leave the office are absolute idiots with a nineteenth-century mentality. If you want to establish power over your peers, value your time and leave early. This is an absolute attention getter. Be fun and pleasant, and then suddenly ask to be excused and leave. This will prevent your peers and superiors from growing tired of your company and they'll always want a little more of you.

- **Say less than necessary, at times:** Some people are inherently verbose, while others are naturally silent, but your comment must meet a certain minimal standard to be considered comprehensive. You leave opportunity for rumination and interpretation by expressing less than required, letting people wonder about you. For example, when someone asks you: 'Are you in a relationship?' what they really expect from you is not just 'yes' or 'no' but the details. A satisfactory answer would be: 'Yes, I am married' or 'Yeah, I got engaged last month.' However, if you merely respond 'Yes' without providing any extra information, the scenario becomes problematic. The other person is interested in you but is hesitant to inquire. When someone asks, 'What do you do for a living?' you can give a broad answer, such as 'I am a businessman,' without going into detail. Many people will want to know more but will be hesitant to ask—partly because they don't want to appear interested, and partly because they don't know what to anticipate from you if they do. This tiny tactic immediately draws people's attention to you.

- **People smell desperation from miles away:** Remember, this book is supposed to teach you to get things through invisible power-play rather than begging. So, please stop begging at work. Think about it this way: if you're overly excited about a work opportunity, that might communicate that you are in low demand. All the more reason to play it cool. Making something harder to get, Professor Jeremy Nicholson says, 'tends to increase at least the perception of the value, if not its actual value.'[19]

Part of making this work means keeping your enthusiasm in check. 'Overeagerness can be a sign of naïveté or sound like plain desperation,'[20] said John Lees, a Britain-based career strategist and the author of *How to Get a Job You Love.*

When it comes to things like compensation negotiations, be clear that you are really interested in finding out more about the opportunity, Mr. Lees suggests, but give a sense that you are aware of your skills and your market value.

---

[19] Jeremy Nicholson, 'Make Them Love You by Taking (Not Giving)', *Psychology Today*, 20 May 2011, https://www.psychologytoday.com/intl/blog/the-attraction-doctor/201105/make-them-love-you-taking-not-giving, Accessed on 9 February 2022.

[20] John Lees, *How to Get a Job You Love*, McGraw-Hill Education, 2016.

If you find yourself approached by hiring managers or potential clients, Dr Nicholson recommends responding in a way that respects their interest without coming across as too eager. In other words, 'You're selective with who you work with, but you would consider working with or for them.'[21]

- **Stop trying so hard to fill pauses:** As my literature teacher always said, 'Pauses are pregnant with meaning.' In a conversation, pauses have their own power. They can provide time for introspection, for the speaker to regain composure, and for the listener's imagination to conjure up anything it wants. It's not always about what you say, but rather what you don't say. When someone asks you to take the metaphorical 'jump', don't be so ready to ask 'how high?' Take your time to respond to demands and requests from other people. Ask yourself—and them—questions about their motives. Tell them you're going to think about it and will get back to them. Ask yourself 'What's the rush?' if someone begs you to answer immediately; and inform them nicely but firmly that you will respond as soon as possible. Allow yourself time to consider possibilities and make informed selections; this is such a lost art for many that it will appear intriguing and alluring.
- **Master a few topics:** When you finally do speak, know exactly what you're saying and charm people out of their rationality.

You're mysterious and intelligent. Since you won't be

---

[21] Jeremy Nicholson, 'Make Them Love You by Taking (Not Giving)', *Psychology Today*, 20 May 2011, https://www.psychologytoday.com/intl/blog/the-attraction-doctor/201105/make-them-love-you-taking-not-giving, Accessed on 9 February 2022.

talking about yourself much, you'll need to learn about some topics that you can talk about at length. Not only does this keep the conversation away from your personal story, it shows that you're passionate enough about a subject to learn it.

Make sure the subject is both intriguing and non-controversial. Presidential candidates, for example, are both interesting and controversial. The environmental impact of farm-produced fish, on the other hand, is intriguing and unlikely to be divisive. It also gives the impression that you care about the environment.

- **Strategic absence is so seductive:** People become overly familiar with you if you are always present, and they may begin to appreciate your presence less and less with time. It helps to make them crave you, even if you wish to create significant partnerships. How can you make them want to be with you? First and foremost, be present and demonstrate your greatness. Practise strategic absence once they've grown to like you and appreciate your company. You're weary, a little preoccupied or, better still, on vacation. You can even go missing without giving a cause (but not too often—you don't want to anger others). They will miss you and inquire about you if you were a lovely person to be around.
- **Stand out:** Enigmatic people are often unpredictable, suddenly voicing an opinion you might have thought to counter their opinions or presence in general. Don't follow the crowd. Instead, look for new ways of seeing and try to think creatively around topics. Ask questions instead of agreeing to avoid conflict.

Play devil's advocate—even if you think they're probably right—or stay silent if three people at a meeting have already spoken up for one way of fixing an issue. It's pointless to add to the chorus of those who are saying the same thing. Ask a lot of questions to make sure you're making the best decisions possible. Clarify, specify and interrogate all ideas to get to the heart of the matter.

- **Your market value is your main weapon:** Keep an updated spreadsheet on hand with a list of your skills and achievements so you can quickly review it when you have an offer. You also have to know how much to charge for your services beforehand. The idea is to plan ahead so you're not scrambling in the moment. Having a firm understanding of how much your skills are worth will allow you to not rush after every opportunity that arises (and yes, this includes hasty email responses.)
- **Short but sweet:** Never say more than what is absolutely necessary. 'Nothing' is an example of a correct response to 'What are you doing after school?' 'I'm going to go home, sit down, read a book, eat supper, and then maybe go shopping,' is the erroneous response. Keep the number of details to a bare minimum.

  You do not, however, have to be harsh or frigid. If someone approaches you and tries to strike up a conversation, be courteous, smile, and respond to their queries (with minimum detail). If they ask any, don't respond if the question makes you uncomfortable. Say you don't want to answer it politely. Think of a candy you know that is super delicious, but you cannot have too much of it. Wouldn't you do almost anything to get some more? Yes, in the workplace, you have to be this candy to gain power and influence over *anyone*.
- **Know thyself, *well*:** Don't confuse being enigmatic around

others with being an enigma to yourself. Self-knowledge is vital to leading a good life and it is something that you need to work on discovering all of your life. Do not neglect this part of your self-care—read widely, keep your thoughts in a journal, be open to new experiences, challenge your fears and misunderstandings, and always be willing to learn.

You know what you like and what you don't like. You know your values, your preferences and what you want in life. You know what your weak spots and insecurities are. This not only makes you sophisticated and trustable but also extremely powerful. It's nearly impossible to manipulate or control a self-aware person, remember? *You* have to take advantage of your peers' lack of self-awareness, but you cannot let them do the same to you. And for that, you have *got to* know yourself inside out.

- **Beware of what you tell your peers:** Remember, you have to elicit information out of them, not give it out yourself. In a world where we're constantly told that we have to speak up or risk never been noticed, too much talking and giving away all of your intent, dreams and desires can result in information overload and stereotyping. The mystery has vanished now that there is nothing more to share, and it can be difficult to modify your peers' and superiors' impressions of you since they've heard too much about who you think you are now. Don't put yourself in a box—be selective about what you tell your peers and supervisors about yourself, and be more giving with those who are closest to you.
- **Stop treating your social media like your personal diary:** Social networking has changed the way we relate to each other, stripping much of the mystery from ourselves. People's impressions of you can be difficult to modify if they've heard

too much about who you think you are now. Don't put yourself in a box online or in-person encounters. Instead, be cautious about what you tell strangers and acquaintances about yourself and more generous with those who are close to you.

Except for those closest to you, there's no need to constantly publicize your locations or your hobbies and tastes in everything. If someone asks where you're going, just evade it saying, 'I'll be around later.'

Remove your location information and status updates from social media sites like Twitter and Facebook. Remove as much personal information as possible from your accounts.

- **Of course, master your tongue:** The mastermind always has a master-tongue and a master-vocabulary. Use unusual colloquialisms. Be creative and say things that will make people sit up and take notice instead of things that will fade into the background of conversations. If someone asks how you're doing, you could say, 'So-so' and be forgotten in an instant. Or, you could say, 'I feel like a long-tailed cat in a room full of rocking chairs.' If someone asks how the baseball game turned out, you could say 'Terrible' or you could say that it was 'Like slurping hot lead.' People will take notice. Build a powerful vocabulary. Spend time every day learning a few new words and practicing them in your conversations. Using precise and accurate diction in your everyday conversations will help you to stand out among the text-talk and chatter. Remember, the most charismatic of leaders and charmers are great orators. Without impressive words and only hard work, you're merely an employee, not an *alpha* employee.

Five Takeaways for You to Skim Over:

- Playing nice is great, but playing too nice all the time is just people-pleasing and you're here to please your own desires, not others.
- Being too available at work makes you a classic pushover who's dumped with tasks and never gets recognition.
- The main secret to being a magnetic person is to leave an element of mystery lingering around you. You always leave people wanting more.
- Mysterious people are alluring—people fight hard to gain the validation of mysterious people. Be a little mysterious, and you'll find others will want to do more and more to impress you. Its basic human nature—we want what we cannot always access.
- Being mysterious also makes you less vulnerable at work—you know your competitors' weaknesses, but they never get to know yours.

6

THE MODERN ALPHA EMPLOYEE

You cannot dream yourself into a character;
you must hammer and forge yourself one.[22]

—James Anthony Froude

Story time again. It was my first day on the job, and I was ready to take the office by storm. I walked into my very first staff meeting and instantly noticed that it wasn't being run by my boss but by another co-worker Travis. This guy really seemed to be in command of the situation, and I was surprised to see the boss (who I really liked) sitting off to the side of the room. When Travis came around to me, I decided to share my 'brilliant idea' that I'd planned to lay on them my very first day. As soon as I uttered my cost savings idea, Travis said: 'God, you're green. That's a stupid idea.' Then the room filled with silence. My pride and enthusiasm were torn to shreds as I instantly realized who the alpha was in the office that day and it wasn't me. However, Travis was more of an old alpha who wouldn't really win in the modern workplace.

---

[22]James Anthony Froude, *The Nemesis Of Faith*, Kessinger Publishing Co, 2004.

- When I started my career, the traditional alpha employee was the professional who dominated the conversations, got their way and crushed the opposition. They'd work their way to the top by self-sacrifice (as well as sacrificing a few careers of others) and make all of this apparent. They were open bull-dozers; open threats.
- To remain the alpha employee in that time, you had to defend yourself daily and that sets off an immense amount of undesirable stress. I can personally remember being afraid to go on vacation because I was concerned that someone would 'steal' my new account right from underneath me or hijack credit for my successful project.

Traditionally, we think of 'alphas' as people who are confident high achievers who get things done. That's great, but folks who embrace this approach to leadership in the workplace frequently lack other important leadership abilities. The modern alpha employee tries to make the power and influence ideal more relevant for today's workforce by incorporating crucial communication skills.

- Modern alpha employees make it seem like they value the fulfilment of others.
- These alpha employees want to have a sense of purpose and significance from their work and they want others to notice.
- Peers and team members may now handle their own duties and solve their own difficulties thanks to new alpha workers. They then praise them for exceptional accomplishment in order to promote positive behaviour. What does that do? It makes these employees hooked to the alpha for more and more validation.

- Modern alpha employees believe in themselves. They lead by example and use self-assuredness and energy to generate excitement, spark ideas and make things happen. They also listen and use the right tools—such as workplace groups—to help them gather feedback.
- The modern alpha employee doesn't focus on getting to the top and then defending their position; instead, they focus on making an impact in their current role and letting the chips fall where they may. When they focus on making an impact where they are, they automatically emerge as leaders and elevate—that too, as the *chosen* leaders.
- Lastly, and most importantly, just like traditional alphas, new alpha employees want to get to the top, but they don't do it by treading on other people's toes *openly*. They know how to fast-track their way up to the top without making everyone in the office want to murder them.

Here are some hacks for you to become the new alpha employee—a wolf everyone follows, knowingly or unknowingly:

Know Your Priorities

List out your top priorities, in addition to work, to see how you should allocate your time and energy. You may prefer to spend time on your hobbies or with your loved ones, so make sure to keep these in mind when scheduling your work week. This also includes your priorities at work. Whether you're trying to earn a promotion or just get through your workload by the end of the week, prioritize the tasks that will help you get there, and be mindful of overextending yourself.

You Should Outshine Your Message

Cambridge scholar, Jochen Menges calls this the 'awestruck effect'. Magnetic leaders and powerful public speakers often have it. Their personal energy is so strong that they could be reading the phone book and you would be captivated. If you walk away from a presentation amazed, but you can't remember the speaker's 2-3 key points, you have been hit by the awestruck effect. Create a personality so dynamic and charming that people take you seriously even if you talk about orange peels or squirrels.

Sweet, Sweet Negotiation

The Alpha doesn't just accept anything on their to-do list. They rarely deal in 'yes' or 'no'. They understand that there's always a window to create a win-win versus win-lose.

Take Risks Every Now and Then

Another important step to be the new alpha employee—one that may seem daunting—is taking risks. I'm not talking about skydiving, unless that's your goal. An ambitious person, on the other hand, is not afraid to take risks and make mistakes. They might, at the end of the day, pay off. Being ambitious entails pursuing your dreams and achieving your objectives. It's about stepping outside of your comfort zone and doing something you've never done before. Being ambitious and taking risks isn't always easy and that's just the idea. But the more you push yourself, the happier you will be and the closer you will be to achieving your ambitious goals.

Learn to put your faith in yourself to attain your goals.

Allow oneself to be open to new possibilities. Even if you make a few errors along the road, it may be a valuable part of the learning process. When you start taking action, you'll notice a difference in your life.

The Power of 'No'

Once you've established your priorities, it's important to exercise your ability to say no at work. For example, if you value taking rest from work on your lunch breaks, politely decline meeting invitations scheduled for that time. Another scenario when it's okay to say no is when you're offered extra work. Consider whether the work will help you directly achieve your goals, and if it doesn't, go ahead and turn it down. Saying no is a powerful skill that helps you enforce your boundaries and keep your goals a priority.

Take Initiative

They move ahead in spite of their own fear to solve the problem plaguing the office. They start *doing* when everyone else is still waiting for permission. Don't worry about not being at the top of the organizational hierarchy; if you feel it's going to lead to success, do it. That is so much more alpha than confusedly waiting for a leader to hold your hand and guide you. Remember, *you* are your own leader.

Set a Safe Distance

When it comes to water cooler talk or happy hours over Zoom, your personal life might get brought up in a professional setting.

It's up to *you* to decide how much personal information you would like to share with co-workers and I suggest you do not share too much.

Let others know that you prefer to stick to conversations about professional topics or if you're open to sharing, be aware that others might not match your communication style. Below are a few examples of what not to share at work.

- Gossip
- Politics
- Religion
- Financial problems
- Intimate/personal problems

Know Your Mentors

The alpha employee identifies strong mentors along the way. They know they have blind spots no matter how far they rise. In order to fast-track through traditional hierarchy, you are to know the ones who will benefit you the most—your superiors. Ask them for feedback, ask them how they got where they are and ask them for a push. Let them know you're in it for the long run and are ambitious.

Embrace Your Ambition

Ambition is a crucial component of accomplishing your goals in life. It can help you stay motivated as you work toward many excellent goals that require hard work and perseverance to obtain. You can start to see your goal and figure out how to make it a reality if you have ambition. Set goals and try to achieve them. Surround yourself with other alpha employees (rather than fighting with them).

When you surround yourself with ambitious people, you may feel more inspired to be motivated yourself. Get to know what habits and thought processes help them be so ambitious. Seek support through networking or by finding a mentor. When choosing a mentor, find someone who is where you want to be. They can help you start working toward this place.

Kill Your Enemies: Self-Doubt and Negativity

Negativity is your adversary, both externally and within. It just serves to hold you back; prevents you from perceiving the positive aspects of life and the opportunities that lie ahead. Negativity spreads a dark shade over your lofty ambitions. It must be ejected. Don't dismantle yourself or your work. Don't measure yourself against others. Work on yourself, your objectives, and what you want to achieve, and keep your eyes on the prize. Your biggest competitor is you, and no one else should take precedence over you. Stop downplaying your efforts; other wolves at work smell your wounds of insecurity from miles away.

Maintain a Confident Persona, Always

Confidence can change the way you're perceived by others and how you see yourself. It can also impact your interactions with others. Even your daily work or mood is subject to your current confidence levels. The new alpha employee isn't a meek prey; they're a wolf who leads the pack. And the leader can never appear jittery or low on self-esteem.

- **Do you have your superhero pose ready?** No, you don't have to put your fist on your hips. But you do have to stand tall. Body language speaks a thousand words. It also goes a long way towards how others perceive confidence.
- **Know their eye colour.** This isn't because their eye colour is important, but by taking a moment to look and make note of it, you will be giving the perfect amount of eye contact. We all know eye contact is important in social situations. Too much is creepy and uncomfortable, and not enough makes us seem shifty and untrustworthy.
- **Be cool as a cucumber at social events.** Do you dislike meeting new people or giving a presentation in front of a large group? Assume you're fine with it. By behaving at ease in any scenario, you can fool your own brain into forgetting about its nervousness. If meeting new people makes you nervous, act as if you already know everyone. You'll appear more relaxed, which will make you more appealing to new acquaintances. It's a win-win situation.
- **Write to-the-point e-mails.** William Shakespeare famously said, 'Brevity is the soul of wit.'[23] It's also the hallmark of honesty and confidence. If you're unsure of what you're saying, you are more likely to ramble. But if you feel 100 per cent certain about something, you'll be able to make your case in as few words as possible.
- **Use that voice.** Voice projection is a speaker's greatest trick. Think of the greatest orators in history. They certainly didn't mumble or pull back.

    You can try the same trick. If you tend to mumble

---

[23] William Shakespeare, *Hamlet*, Fingerprint! Publishing, 2015.

when you're nervous, play with projection. Speak a little louder than you normally would. It can help you come across as more confident.
- **Make your confidence contagious.** Who doesn't like to hang out with people who make them feel good about themselves? One sign of a true friend is that they see your best qualities and help you see them too. A talented charmer uses this same ability to lower defences. It is possible for your peers to become addicted to your praise and approval, and they will do *anything* to get it.
- **Accept compliments *humbly*.** Do you think Steve Jobs responded to praise with, 'Aw, no, you're so sweet, but I really messed up that one product-launch?' No. He smiles beamingly, says a gracious 'Thank you,' and continues on—knowing the compliment was 100 per cent true and that his mere presence gives everyone around him excitement. Basically, the secret to faking confidence is asking yourself: what would my favourite leader do?
- **Walk fast.** Walking briskly can indicate to other people that you are confident. Walking briskly will cause you to stand upright and erect as well.

  A quick pace indicates that you have a purpose for moving, that you are focused and driven to complete a task. A slower speed indicates that you are less ambitious and have less motivation to move. The former certainly comes across as more self-assured. Ever seen the greatest leaders drag themselves across the red carpet?
- **Dress to kill.** You may hear that you should dress for the job you want, not the job you have. This is a power play that helps boost your confidence levels. But it works in different

situations, too. The key factor is that you dress the part. If you wear things that make you look good, you'll also feel good. So, put on clothing that makes you feel confident. Furthermore, you don't have to break the bank to overhaul your wardrobe. Confidence-boosting accessories like a great pair of shoes or bold jewellery also do the trick. But don't stop at your clothing. Take a look at your entire look. From your hair to your shoes, make sure they all help you feel confident. Otherwise, the smallest thing may throw you off.

- **Stop fidgeting.** Tap, tap, tap. Swivel, swivel. Bounce, bounce. All those unconscious nervous habits you have—tapping on the table, swivelling in your chair or bouncing your foot under the desk are dead giveaways for nervousness. They also amplify your anxiety.
- **Lower your pitch.** When you're not confident and a bit nervous, your voice tends to sound high-pitched. It's not always easy to detect when it's happening. Whether you realize you talk in a high voice or not, make a conscious effort to keep your voice a little lower. Pay attention to how your voice changes if you're feeling uneasy. If you're having trouble hearing yourself, lower the pitch of your voice as well as the volume. To put it another way, speak up. This will demonstrate to others that you believe your voice is important enough to be heard. Then they'll be more likely to think the same way as you.
- **Talk about what makes you passionate.** Try to talk about subjects which you know well and which you have an interest in. Enthusiasm often comes across as confidence. If you don't know much about the conversation topic, don't panic. Just ask some questions. Many people love talking, especially

> about the areas which they are knowledgeable in. They will be more than happy to share their information and experiences with you. It also makes them feel wanted, and makes you irresistible to them. Voila, you're the modern alpha employee!

Five Takeaways for You to Skim Over:

- The modern alpha employee knows what they want and knows very well how to work towards it. They don't just sit around waiting for rewards or power. They earn it.
- The modern alpha employee is passionate, smart, powerful and mostly, ambitious.
- The modern alpha employee has the aura of a leader even if they are low in a company's organizational position.
- The modern alpha employee is charming but isn't a people-pleaser or a weakling. They know how to create a safe distance and prioritize their own career and ambition first.
- The modern alpha employee doesn't trust anyone at work fully, but keeps their company's hierarchal alphas close. They gain the favour of his superiors and turn them into mentors.

7

DYNAMIC DIPLOMACY

*Tact is the art of making a point
without making an enemy.*

—Isaac Newton

A colleague of yours, Terry, is asked to take the lead on an extensive project which you will be working on over the course of several months. Your team meets several times to get your initial ideas together and prepare a presentation for your supervisor. You feel confident that the group's ideas are thorough and well-researched. At the meeting, you are baffled by Terry's presentation. You had put a significant amount of work into the project and yet your ideas appear to have been completely cut out! Instead, Terry has replaced them with his own ideas which were not agreed upon by the group. Immediately after the presentation, your supervisor asks you to address some concerns they have, and you are not surprised as they are the same concerns you had initially presented to Terry.

You feel betrayed and enraged, so you launch into an emotional outburst about how you have been cut out from the project, you don't even agree with the ideas in the presentation and lash out against Terry. He's a clear enemy, isn't he? Yes, however, your bigger enemies are your emotions—look what they just did. Your supervisor is appalled by your unprofessional behaviour and scraps the project completely.

While your feelings might be justified, a clever response without diplomacy is plain foolish. You play mind games; you don't let *your own* mind succumb to others' games. Remember that throughout, especially when you know you have to keep dealing with Terry and your boss.

There are *countless* people you must work with every day, from your business managers, your bosses, to your colleagues, and everyone in-between. Let's just say they're not the easiest to coexist with. Being diplomatic basically lets you have your way without creating out-and-out enemies—you make them feel like they're winning when, in reality, *you* are.

Imagine you need some new equipment for your office space, whatever it may be. Consider specifically *what* you need and the kind of help needed to install it. Speak to your supervisor and outline your request, then ask if it is a possibility. If yes, take the next steps to ensure that the *right* people are willing and able to help you. Talk with these individuals, convince them they also profit from this new equipment equally, and wait for their response. You already know: people feel validated when you admit you aren't able to do everything yourself and want their expertise on a subject you know little about.

If they say no, you re-evaluate your request. Remember, the request is the same, but it's the words that are different. Sometimes, it is all about baby steps and making sure that a *seeming* trust is established between all those involved.

Tact is being able to share your thoughts and needs in a way that makes it seem you have considered other people's feelings and reactions. Remember, you want to have your way by making others feel they're having theirs. No one wants to hear they did something wrong—even less if it's coming from a boss who doesn't seem to care about how they're delivering that feedback. Having tact makes people see that you have character, are professional and mature. It's the key to playing a nice guy at work to climb the corporate ladder. All these things are needed to build a good reputation which then creates trust and charisma. See these examples for yourself:

- Your boss asks you to take on some of her workload, so that she can leave early on Friday. However, your schedule is full and you're not sure you'll get everything done on time. A clever, diplomatic response might be, 'Thank you for trusting me with some of your responsibilities. I'm sorry that I can't help you this time because of my workload. Is there anything I could help you with next week, when I have more time?'
- Sally, one of your team members, is frequently late for work, which has a negative impact on her performance. You're tempted to call Sally out in the staff meeting after yet another missed deadline. While this may make you feel better in the short term, it is detrimental to your attractive 'nice-guy' image. A more sensible strategy would be to talk to her privately about her tardiness. Even if you're boiling with rage on the inside, you could start with a seemingly kind approach. For example, 'I've noticed you've had trouble getting to work on time. What can I do to help?' is so much better to remain in everyone's good books than blurting out, 'Why the heck are you always late, Sally?'

How Do You Remain in Everyone's Good Books While Always Getting Your Way?

- **At times, borrow a little power.** When presenting a concept to someone in a position of authority over you, such as your boss, a successful businessperson or any other type of leader, being able to take part of their power away can help persuade them to understand your point of view.

    The whole idea is that many people with power know that they're powerful and tend to look down on people who are of a lesser position. However, you can take away some of their power by exposing them to new experiences; by including material that they are unlikely to be familiar with, you can quietly show them that you are more knowledgeable than they are on the subject you're discussing. They will feel less powerful if you are more aware about the subject. Then, near the end of the conversation, remind them of their power position to give them more confidence in their evaluation of your proposal. That way, you become their boss in that moment, yet they feel like the bosses.

- **Manipulate timing and setting.** A good diplomat remains alert to the 'right moments' to 'make hay while the sun shines'. Leverage current affairs (not the big world affairs, but the affairs inside your organization) to know when to make your move. The other aspect of 'setting' is choosing the right ambience for your talk. The *European Journal of Social Psychology* says that this simple act can impact your negotiation outcome by 40 per cent. Choose what emotions you want to convey during that deal:

- A formal oval-office setting makes a more intimidating impression of power (works best for wall-street style deals, lawyers, etc.).
- An elegant dinner environment spells sophistication and openness to interaction (new-client wins, fashion and luxury markets, etc.).
- A relaxing coffee-talk in a cafe works best to induce comfort, ease stiffness and makes you appear more friendly (works well for creative ventures such as advertising, design, coaching and training topics, etc.).

- **Let something little go.** There will be times when two people, with conflicting ideas, make compelling arguments for objectives that are in direct opposition to one another. When such a situation arises, you will need to negotiate, and you may need to make sacrifices (that don't really matter to you) to reach an agreement. You merely make it seem like you're making a huge sacrifice for their benefit.

  A mutual sacrifice is an effective tool for reaching a resolution, even when one party must give up more than the other. Agreeing to a small sacrifice (however, make it seem big) can establish a sense of camaraderie and prove that your focus is on resolution and not 'winning'. When possible, look for a compromise that allows everyone involved to feel the benefit of the results.

- **Do not gossip openly; it's corporate suicide.** Your colleague is known as the office gossip, and he's spreading rumours about another colleague when you're in the room. What's your role? To play the hero—the nice guy who remains in everyone's good books. That way, you're never seen as a threat yet you have dirt on all your gossipy peers.

For instance, say something positive (even if you don't mean it) with a lot of firmness and emotion: 'Mac might struggle with her sales figures, but she's a hard worker.' Or, ask them to stop: 'I don't want to talk about this, especially since we don't know the facts. Let's discuss the upcoming merger instead.' (makes you seem like Jesus Christ, doesn't it?)

You can also say, 'I don't want to talk about people behind their backs,' or 'Let's talk about this when Mac is here so that she can address these issues.' What happens next? *Everyone* trusts you and everyone is vulnerable to being controlled by you without them even realizing it.

- **Shoot from a distance, *indirectly*.** Sometimes, direct attack doesn't work. We may have to address the issue a little sneakily. For example, if you are not happy with a certain new plan at work regarding budget distribution, gather facts to divert attention. You can create a convincing presentation showing how profits, employee-retention and customer-satisfaction is being adversely affected by undertaking that new plan; so that you are shifting focus deliberately from budget to another topic such as employee retention. This will help people see differently—by leveraging a wider range of facts and emotions. It is like changing topics in a conversation that is not going your way.
- **A little fear goes a long way.** Research suggests that people, who experience anxiety and then a sense of relief, usually respond positively to requests afterward. People who heard an unseen police officer's whistle while crossing the street, for example, were more likely to consent to fill out a questionnaire than those who did not. That could be

because their cognitive resources were diverted to pondering the potential threat they had faced, leaving them with fewer resources to consider the request that had just been made.

Blowing a whistle in the midst of your office is generally not a good idea. Consider gently frightening a co-worker by reminding them of a project coming later that day (Just kidding! It's due tomorrow) and then asking whether they'd be willing to assist you.

- **Your palms should be nice and warm.** We all know that a good handshake is important. It can't be too weak or it'll break your bones, and no one wants sweating hands. Did you realize, though, that chilly hands make a poor first impression? When meeting new individuals, make sure your hands are warm. If your hands are frequently cold, a brief trip to the lavatory to wash them in warm water should suffice.

- **Open your mouth carefully.** Your choice of words can influence how others perceive your message. Avoid starting sentences with the word 'you'. 'You need to do better next time,' for example, will make the other person defensive. Instead, use softer, more indirect language like, 'I think your presentation would be greater if you spent more time researching next time.'

When you're in a fight or giving constructive criticism, it's very vital to employ 'I' phrases. Instead of blaming yourself, you take responsibility for your feelings. 'I view it differently,' for example, or 'I had to read that passage numerous times before I comprehended your point.'

When you disagree with someone, you can employ a 'cushion' or connecting comment. 'You're wrong, our team did great last quarter,' for example, can be softened with 'I appreciate your opinion, but our team did well last quarter.' Also, be succinct when speaking in a heated situation. When you're uncomfortable, it's tempting to keep talking, which raises the chances that you'll say too much or say something you'll regret. Only express what you need to say, and be honest and assertive.

- **Cool as a cucumber.** If someone tries to loudly talk over you, just keep talking. But here's the secret: don't change your cadence or raise your voice at all. Just keep speaking like you were before they tried to interrupt you. They'll be uncomfortable and they'll most likely back down. You're still the nice man, and they're the new workplace jerks. One enemy down.
- **At times, pick up the pace during an argument.** How you communicate your ideas can be just as important as the substance of your argument. Research suggests that when someone disagrees with you, you should speak faster so they have less time to process what you're saying. On the contrary, when you're delivering an argument that your audience agrees with, it helps to speak more slowly, so they have time to evaluate the message. Speak faster, but remain soft and gentle—its hypnotic.
- **And of course, at times, let the whiny work-child win (especially if there's an audience).** Simply be nice, cooperative and upbeat if someone tries to engage you in a debate. When they try to motivate you, smile, shrug and reply, 'Perhaps you're right.' Nothing can knock the wind out of a jerk's sails faster than a jerk's sails. You save your time, energy and your image—you also leave your opponent either infuriated, baffled or charmed. You only win when you *let* them win.

- **Don't ask people for help, ask *one person*.** When help is thrown out to a large group of people, no one will respond. But asking individuals? Well, that makes the help much harder to refuse. So, don't ask your entire office if anyone can lend you a hand moving this weekend—ask just Jerry in Accounting. (Plus, Jerry just likes to be made to feel special, even if he isn't. Ugly truth!)
- **The power of positive language.** Clear, smart vocabulary can change your game. For example, let's say your autocratic boss has been micro-managing you, and you just need some room to breathe. Start by saying: 'I appreciate all your support. Your inputs are insightful. I have been thinking about shouldering more responsibility, however. That way, we can both free up creative space for efficiency.' This is a lot more effective than getting spiteful with your manager. Ego needs to take a step back. You can have your way without compromising self-esteem just by shifting the vocabulary and tone of voice.
- **Test the waters.** When a group of people laugh together, each person instinctively glances at the person within the group they feel most connected with. Want to know who is secretly sleeping together, or who is on the top or bottom of the social hierarchy? Check out where everyone glances next time something hilarious happens. If you cannot convince your boss, get through to them by charming their favourite peer—the one they always look at when they have a good old laugh. Nobody is useless in the office to a mind-controller; anyone and everyone can be used as a means to get what they want.
- **Your excitement spreads like the plague.** If you want others to jump on board with a concept, be as enthusiastic as

possible about it. Show your excitement to see someone if you want them to be excited to see you. Everyone is taken in by the dog who is ecstatic to see his owner return. Don't be that dog. People will reciprocate your joy if you show it. You will have your way in the most diplomatic manner.

- **Ask when they're weak.** An alert mind may express some doubts when approached with a request. Someone who is weary or distracted, on the other hand, is likely to be less critical and take what you say as true. So, if you're going to ask a co-worker for assistance with a project, do so towards the end of the day. That way, they will be drained from the day's tasks and won't have the mental energy to realize that they'd rather be doing something else.
- **Gently push others to say *your* idea.** If you know you are going to be pitching a notoriously hard-to-sell person, it's better to hold off presenting your whole package and instead open up a discussion in which you gently nudge her toward your plan.

The best way to do this is to start the conversation by gently stating your goal but then opening up the floor to questions and alternatives. Phrases like 'What do you think about this?' or 'What sorts of solutions did you have in mind?' help you get a better sense of the other person's perspective. You can then guide the discussion down your path by replying with 'What you do think about us doing X?' or 'I was thinking about X, how does that sound?'

During the conversation, you also want to stay on top of validating the other person's ideas. No need to proclaim their solutions as 'the best idea ever!' but offering positive feedback such as, 'I think that is a good solution' or 'That is really original, I didn't think of that' helps make them feel good and eventually become more receptive toward accepting your ideas.

- **Always pretend to stand for a higher cause.** Imagine there are two homeless guys standing on a street corner. The first guy has a normal, run-of-the-mill sign saying, 'Spare a few dollars? God bless you.' The second guy, on the other hand, has a much more unusual sign: 'Can't afford to feed my family, and it's tearing me apart. Please help, so I can stop feeling like such an awful Dad.'

    Which one would you be more likely to help? The second one, right? Forget giving him a few bucks. With a sign like that, you'd take him to the grocery store and buy him $200 worth of groceries. I know *I* would.

    That's the power of standing for something bigger than yourself. It makes people care; it makes people want to do whatever you want them to.

- **'No pressure.'** It might sound counterintuitive, but reminding people that they have the option not to do what you want can often motivate them to oblige your request. The exact phrasing doesn't matter so much; you can say something as simple as, 'But obviously do not feel obliged.' That way, you make them feel like they had a complete say in something when, in reality, they were being subtly controlled by you. Yes, now you know how a democratic country works.

- **'Let's get started!'** Working on a group project? If you want someone to do something, start by asking them, 'Can you get started on this?' Getting started on something sounds like less work than actually completing a task, but chances are, once they've gotten started, they'll go ahead and finish it.

- **Repeat. Repeat. And repeat again.** Have you ever heard a song for the first time and not really liked it, only to come to love it later after hearing it several more times? Because the human brain thrives on repetition and patterns, when we are frequently exposed to an idea, we are more likely to appreciate or accept it than when we initially heard it. Repeat the relevant facts two or three times while pitching an idea or notion. If you want to persuade someone of a product's quality, for example, compare its efficacy figures to those of other similar products. If you're having a friendly debate with a friend or co-worker, keep repeating a point in different ways throughout your conversation. They may not realize they've heard the same thing multiple times, but their brain will pick up on it and they'll be more likely to see your point of view. In this sort of situation, it's good to keep it to three times; if it's obviously the same information repeated multiple times—rather than being subtly transformed with the same core idea—it can actually cause the opposite effect and leave the person feeling more resistant to it.

- **Reveal loopholes before they can.** Very few ideas are perfect; even the best plans, concepts and views can have a flaw or two. While you may believe that the greatest method to persuade someone is to focus solely on the benefits while attempting to obscure any potential disadvantages, research has shown that balanced arguments are the most effective. When presented with a concept, many individuals will hunt for flaws. They may perceive you as deceptive if you do not acknowledge evident shortcomings. People aren't nearly as foolish as we believe.

If they don't see the flaws but think your proposal is too wonderful to be true, they'll have a hard time trusting you and will be difficult to convince. People are only drawn

to those whom they feel they can trust and are more likely to listen to you if you come off that way. Don't make your ideas 'too good to be true.'
- **Act like you *always* have a purpose.** You can get very far in life if you're holding a clipboard and walking with purpose. Nobody thinks to stop the person with a clipboard who clearly is in the middle of an important task. Take advantage of it.
- **The last isn't the least.** If you want someone to choose a specific option, give them a list of three choices and put the one you want them to pick last. They'll be more likely to choose that one since it's freshest in their mind. The next you want your co-worker to pick the lamest of tasks in the project, present it as the last option and they might just willingly agree to get their hands dirty.
- **Randomly insert praises to be tactful.** Obviously, people like to be complimented; so yes, tell whoever you're talking to that their shoes are working for you. But also, research indicates that speaking positively of a third party makes you look confident. And that makes sense if you think about it in reverse—don't people seem super not confident when they trash other people?
- **Be specific.** People like having a choice; if you want something, you will have more success if you give people choices. Rather than asking, 'Would you like to contribute to this project?' try 'Would you like to make a small contribution through proofreading or content writing? You know what's best for you!' with a nice smile, and they won't say no.
- **Kill the jokester.** You know how a joke ceases to be funny when you have to repeat it? Use that to your benefit. Act

as if you can't hear him and politely ask him to repeat it three times if a peer in the group is making jokes about you and putting you down. No one is laughing by the third or fourth time he repeats it.

Who's laughing now? Not him, most definitely.

- **Pull your enemy closer.** If you expect to have a conflict with someone, seat yourself next to that person rather than across from them. Your position is less oppositional, and the person next to you is less likely to feel as threatened. This technique is handy to remember in conference rooms or even at your Thanksgiving table.
- **Ask for an inch, take a mile.** You've probably heard the expression, 'Give them an inch, and they'll take a mile.' It's meant to be insulting. It's meant to be a cautionary tale about appeasement. Its purpose is to keep you safe from being taken advantage of. But it's also a terrific way to keep your thinking in check.

Whenever you're asking for anything, never start by asking for everything upfront. Start small instead. Make it simple for people to get started. If it doesn't work out, lower the risk. Allow them to see the outcomes for themselves. And if it goes well, request more. And there's more and more. You may believe it is unethical, but if things are going well, why not press for more? It isn't a case of duplicity. It's a matter of common sense.

- If you want to write a guest post for a prominent site, propose the concept in one or two lines, then email them an outline and then compose the entire post.
- If you want to undertake a joint venture with a thought leader in your sector, start by requesting them to email your

> launch content to 10 per cent of their list, then 50 per cent, then 100 per cent and finally a direct mail campaign.
> - If you want your clients to write case studies for you, start with a 1-3 sentence blurb, then a half-page testimonial and then speak about having a two-hour webinar on their success.

- **Power-terms.** Some words are more persuasive than others. Words known as 'power terms' can be incorporated into your argument or pitch to persuade more effectively. They're grouped into three categories: god terms, devil terms, and charismatic terms.

    'God terms' are also known as power words and tend to be positive and attractive. For example, if you're talking about safety, some associated god words are 'guarantee' and 'proven'.

    On the other hand, 'devil words' are more negative and repulsive to audiences. With the same examples on safety, a couple that can be used are 'dangerous' and 'risky'.

    Then, there are 'charismatic terms' which are a bit trickier. They're usually fairly abstract but appealing because of historical context—words like 'freedom' or 'progress'. Any of the words in these categories can help sway the way people think and feel about a concept or viewpoint. They prompt specific reactions because we've been programmed through experience over the course of our lives to perceive these words a certain way. You can use these types of words to create appeal and draw someone in or to make an alternate option seem undesirable.

- **Don't *ever* succumb to emotions.** Raving like a lunatic is a poor way to convince anyone you're right. Being confident

in the facts that you're presenting, in the evidence you're using to support your claims and in the perspective you're bringing to the table will make it easy for anyone to be convinced of your points.
- **Lastly, know when to back off.** Clever mind-controllers bring you along in your own time and they give you the space and time to carefully consider their position.

    You ought to know that nothing is more powerful than someone persuading themselves on your behalf. That almost never occurs in the presence of the persuader, which is you. Give them space to let your mind-control work its magic in isolation.

The next time you want to persuade someone of something truly important, follow the tips above, make your case and walk away. They will most likely follow because they like you for not being desperate, aggressive or pushy.

Here Are Some Quick Hacks to Maintain the Nice-Guy Act During a Workplace Dispute:

- The first thing to do is **let them argue while you *debate*.** Try to stay calm and say, 'That's interesting.' Then give yourself a moment to think. If they ask why you're silent, say 'I'm giving what you said some thought.' It'll show that you respect their opinion even if you don't. And I *know* you don't.
- Your body language can make a huge difference in an argument. **Maintain a tall and poised stance**, but refrain from using aggressive body language such as crossing your arms, clenched fists or tapping your feet. Your nice-guy

image will be ruined by hostile body language, which is exactly what you need to accomplish what you want.
- **Only say something when you're *absolutely* sure about what you want to say.** The opponent may try to provoke you. Don't just argue for the sake of argument. Otherwise, just shut up, and always remain in your turf.
- If they get aggressive, you **get playfully sarcastic.** End your conversation with sarcasm like 'I guess I am the total idiot here. Thanks for educating me, Ned!' I know I sound childish, but this works! This gets on their nerves more than anything else.
- **Breathe it out.** When you feel like your lid is about to blow, take a long, deep breath. Deep breathing releases tension, calms down our fight-or-flight reactions and allows us to quieten our anxious nerves so that we choose more considerate and constructive responses, no matter the situation.
- **Show compassion when there is an audience.** Remember, *show*. You could be wanting to kill someone on the inside, but you have to act like you empathize. Laugh it off after an argument and playfully flaunt your empathy. Your audience loves watching a good guy as the main character.

- 'That person is frustrated just like me at times!'
- 'He can be slightly impatient, just like me at times.'
- 'We all have our bad days. It's okay if she is being a little cold.'
- 'I wonder if something is stressing him. He's been a little aggressive since the last couple of days and I honestly understand.'

- If someone says something you think is totally incorrect, rather than openly saying they're wrong, **start asking open-**

ended, vague questions. Don't do it in an abrasive way, just start exploring their position. If they are wrong, you will expose it through your questioning. You politely lead them to their grave without having to push them and you get brownie points for pretending to understand their standpoint.
- This is a psychological tactic, which involves causing the opponent to think they're winning the battle. The result is that the opponent will lower their guard. Don't waste time. Hit the opponent so hard below the belt by asking them an unexpected question they can't answer. You'll know the opponent is frustrated when they start fumbling awkwardly with the question until they have no choice but to get annoyed. Have no regard at this point. Hit the opponent below the belt—again and again. You'll know the opponent is defeated when they change their face, have nothing more to say and get evidently annoyed. By this time, your opponent has no choice but take flight.

Five Takeaways for You to Skim Over:

- Conflict and arguments to the office are like trees to a jungle. They're everywhere. The nice charmer always plays it diplomatic to have only allies and no enemies.
- Tact isn't so much about what you ask for but *how* you ask for it. Ask nicely, cleverly and you can get almost *anything*.
- You also have to know when you have to ask for something; and where. Yes, these things matter equally.
- Don't lose your precious nice guy persona even during an argument. You have an audience and in order to be their hero, you have to play the part.
- Handle enemies diplomatically. Kill them with kindness,

remain calm, ask open-ended questions to make them feel you're trying to understand them when, in reality, you're only trying to confuse them. You get the gist.

8

POWER-PLAY LIKE A PRO

The supreme art of war is to subdue the enemy without fighting.[24]

—Sun Tzu, military strategist, philosopher and author of *The Art of War*

Organizational politics is inescapable. A few years ago, I was sharing this reality with a group of young managers. One of the delegates, James, was visibly concerned by what I was saying, and so I asked him to share what he was thinking.

'I'm really struggling with accepting the fact that there is never going to be a place where I won't be dealing with politics. Surely, there must be somewhere?' James pondered.

'Like where?' I asked.

'Well, what about NGOs? Or a church? You know—places where people work for the greater good of the world. Surely, there is no politics there.'

I suppressed a laugh and by way of an answer, told James the story of a friend of mine, Jessica who had been a church

---

[24] Sun Tzu, *The Art of War*, Jaico Publishing House, 2010.

minister. After having led a congregation for about 10 years, she decided to get into business. The one thing that really concerned Jessica while transitioning was the dreaded 'corporate politics' she was warned about by her colleagues and saw repeated complaints from her friends in business. Undeterred, but still quite nervous, she made the leap into a big auditing firm and after a few months, I couldn't wait to find out how it was going.

'I'm loving it,' Jessica told me over coffee.

'What about the politics? Are you coping?' I asked her, concerned and intrigued.

'Politics? Are you kidding me? Corporate politics is *absolutely nothing* compared to church politics!'

Yep, politics is everywhere, no matter what your work is. Politics is a dirty term, but politics in the office is nonetheless unavoidable. As Aristotle noted, 'Man is by nature a political animal.'[25] Whether one participates in them or not, politics bears big influence over what happens to them, their projects and their team. So, it's hard to be indifferent to them.

To borrow from the political scientist, Harold Laswell, office politics can be understood as the unwritten rules that determine who gets what, when and how—a promotion, a budget for a project, a say in the boss's decisions—and who doesn't.[26] This is why most people hate politics: when our fate depends on unwritten rules, things are bound to be arbitrary and unfair; but

---

[25] Aristotle, *The Politics*, Penguin Classics, 1981.

[26] Robert B. (Rob) Kaiser, Tomas Chamorro-Premuzic and Derek Lusk, 'Playing Office Politics Without Selling Your Soul', *Harvard Business Review*, 14 September 2017, https://hbr.org/2017/09/playing-office-politics-without-selling-your-soul?utm_medium=social&utm_source=facebook&utm_campaign=hbr, Accessed on 9 February 2022.

not for the master charmer. The master charmer uses these politics to his/her advantage rather than avoiding them like the plague.

We've all been there. There's that one boss or co-worker who makes your life a living nightmare. It could be that your boss is a compulsive liar or has favourites on the team. It could also be that you have problems with the corporate culture and its rigid rules that must be followed exactly for your work to be 'acceptable'.

What comes to mind when you hear the words 'office politics?' Is it majorly 'backstabbing', spreading rumours and 'sucking up' to the important people? If so, you would want to stay as far away from it as possible. But, whether you like or loathe it, office politics is a fact of life in any organization. And you got to do all of these things as sneakily and subtly as possible.

For example, let's say you have a big meeting coming up where stakeholders at your company are going to decide which projects to invest in—including yours. If you're attuned to politics, you know that to get your project green-lighted, you need to first understand the priorities as well as the perspectives of those stakeholders. You need to confer with them beforehand. Learn what they are looking out for so that you can be more persuasive in presenting your idea. This is an idea of how office politics can be ethically put to use to help you gain an advantage. Look? You're not really murdering anyone or anything.

How Do You Play the Politics to Win, *Always*?

- **Observe the battleground.** Observe every interpersonal dynamic, every reaction, every word choice, every detail and tone on who receives what, every decision and allocation of resources.

> **Decisions:** Watch how decisions are made, how transparent and fair they seem to be. Are they announced in a straight-forward way?
>
> **Details and Tones:** Both in meetings and conversations you are involved with and the ones you overhear, listen to both words and their inference. You'll learn about those people and you might hear things that help you.
>
> **Who Receives What?** Track who gets sent to fun or high-profile conferences and who gets plum assignments. Look for any patterns. For example: are they going to the same people over and over? Are they going to the people with the most appropriate expertise or portfolio? If not, there's something else going on. Who has influence?

- **Know the dynamics.** Whether you just started a new job or just realized that avoiding office politics is detrimental to your career, you have to begin by figuring out exactly what's going on. Your office is full of allies and rivals, and if you watch and listen closely, you can get a pretty good sense of who's aligned with whom:

> - Who has lunch together?
> - Who gets invited to important meetings, and who doesn't?
> - Who always seems to be the first to know about coming changes, and who always seems to be last to know?
> - What are the hot buttons that get tempers boiling?
> - Who hates whom?

The answers to these questions define your battlefield. This doesn't mean that you should be aligned to one side—which would be counterproductive—but it's smart to first understand the rules along with the players and their strategies before you jump into the fray. Otherwise, you could find yourself unintentionally caught up in a long, simmering rivalry! To be the nice guy, you must always play nice.

- **Kiss up to the powerful ones every now and then.** Everyone likes to have nice things said about them, especially difficult people. They like their egos stroked, so just do it! Sure, it's fake. You're probably thinking that you shouldn't have to stoop to that level just to get along with problematic people. However, if this problem person is your boss, you have no choice. I have been in situations where some people don't have a filter for their dislike of their boss (or co-workers). It does not turn out pretty. So, learn to fake it. It may not sound like a great thing to do, but it's the only thing you can do to win in office politics, especially if the person is your superior.

- **The golden time and golden opportunity.** Don't be forceful with opportunities. Instead, welcome them while keeping your eyes open. If you've been waiting to pitch something to your boss, don't force the conversation. This may mean waiting for weeks before you get a good chance, but once you get it, don't miss it. When we encounter a person with, for instance, a proposal, half the battle is already won or lost depending on their mood in the moment.

- ***Do not* share personal opinions.** If you want to use office politics for positive benefits, it is important that you keep any and all of your opinions about colleagues to yourself. The moment you share them with a team member or with the wider organization, you will start to lose your influence as a nice person. Everything you say in the office can be used against you by your opponents. Mental politics should never become verbal.

- **Know your pawns.** You cannot play the game if you don't know its characters inside out! Rely on people's psychological needs and use them as a pressure point. This might be a need to belong, to be accepted or included or the complete opposite—the need to stand out and swim against the current.

    The risky decision-maker can be convinced into making a poor decision, the quiet introvert can be discouraged from pursuing *anything* that would lead them to not conform; it's all in your hands!

    Their weakness is your strength, it's just a matter of figuring out how to harness that to your advantage. Are they prone to overconfidence that will eventually make them stumble? Are they insecure about something or the other which can help your cause in convincing them? Everyone has their kryptonite.

    The more you learn about someone's psychology, thoughts and characteristics, the more advantage you can gain over their thinking and your overall influence on said thoughts. The key to success here is *knowledge*.

- **Trust less, trust with caution.** Trusting others isn't always a good thing. Trust me, I know. Sit back and assess people and their personalities. Listen to their words, and more importantly, observe their behaviour. Practise caution while sharing information, particularly if it's negative. Everyone you interact with should be seen as a potential spy who might leak information to the enemy. It sounds cynical, but ultimately is self-preservation. Hopefully, you have true friends you can trust in the workplace, but don't go around sharing your thoughts and feelings too freely.

One of the trickiest parts of working in an office is conducting yourself professionally in social situations at work events. While the company party presents as the perfect chance for you to kick back with a few beers and enjoy yourself, it's vital to keep in mind that one wrong comment in a relaxed setting could ruin the rapport you've spent all year building. Informal environments are a lie—everything you say can be used against you.

- **You have to appear to be sincere, always**. Seeming to be honest, open and forthright is your main ammunition in this bloody war. It is not enough to just be honest; sincerity is in the eye of the beholder. How honest you think you are will be far less important than how honest other people think you are. Don't go around saying bad things about your bosses; don't reveal your ambitions; don't tell your peers why you are so nice to each and every superior. Keep your strategies to yourself.
- **Your body must match your fakery.** Actions speak louder than words. This can be backed-up by research. If some verbal information ('I think you are awesome!') is accompanied by negative body-language (eye-rolling or scowls on your face), the person will always believe your non-verbal message over others. It's quite hard to control your body-language because it's tied to your emotions. You must make an effort to be aware of what you are saying with your body. Smile. Nod. Tilt your head. Laugh. 'Fake it till you make it!'
- **Forge a win-win.** You'll also need to keep things win-win, even though that's not really possible. Thinking that you

only win if your opponent limps off the battlefield, bloody and bruised is old-school. But done correctly, office politics isn't a zero-sum game. Navigating office politics works best when you follow the golden rule of negotiating: end with everybody *feeling* like they won. In place of making efforts to take down your competitor, spend that time and energy coming up ways for both to benefit. This is how you play the game smart.

- **Make everyone believe you're an ally.** Most people long for someone to say, 'I get what you're saying,' 'You're absolutely right,' or 'You deserve better' whether it's at work or beyond it. It's human nature.

    This is especially true when a feeling of injustice or unfairness is involved. Charismatic people know that a little empathy goes a *long* way. Many people are satisfied just hearing 'I'm on your side' without seeing any behaviour to back up that claim. Swear over and over that you understand and support your peers; they won't usually measure your actions against your pretty words.

- **Tweak their perspective.** Cloak the reality of those you're attempting to manipulate with a reality that you've weaved— go matrix on their minds! This one's about tact, cunning ability and, most importantly, hypnotic and seductive language.

    Put thought into how your arguments are structured and delivered, whether they appeal to someone's emotion or logic. Do you come across sounding like you know what you're talking about even when you don't? If you can't persuade someone to quit wasting paper for environmental reasons, can you persuade them that less paper means less work with a perfectly valid argument? Thinking outside the box and re-framing a perspective on any given scenario can help you see things more clearly and improve the effectiveness of any argument you make.

- **Have your foot in *each* side.** One of the smartest things you can do is to build alliances throughout the company so that you'll have a foot in as many of the political camps as possible. You'll have a decent chance of coming out ahead if you accomplish this and demonstrate people across the board that they can count on you, regardless of whose political side is now 'winning'. You also won't be left out in the cold if a group of allies leaves the company.
- **Lastly, no trash-talking, whatsoever.** It's tempting to trash someone you're competing for a promotion against while they're not around, but speaking negatively about your co-workers can do more harm than good. People are smart enough to figure out that if you tell them something negative about one of their co-workers, you'll probably do the same to them. When you refuse to engage in a conversation where you could be tempted to gossip about a co-worker, you send a very powerful message that you can be trusted in the opposite direction as well.

And when it comes to speaking negatively about those in power, it's best to be *very, very* careful. These are ones who give you what you want. Just assume everything you say at work will be heard by the boss.

Speaking of what you say, let me go a little into the magic of hypnotic language. When it comes to hypnosis, one tool is more powerful than all the others put together. You might even say that, without it, hypnosis would be impossible. And that tool is: words.

Sounds simple, doesn't it? You only need to be able to utilize words to be a hypnotist. That is something that anyone can do. So, why isn't everyone capable of hypnotizing others? They aren't just any words, after all. Master charmers employ precise words and phrases to assist individuals in imagining possibilities, which necessitates careful word selection. Those powerful words are referred to as 'power words' by us (or hypnotic power words).

But here's the thing: power words aren't that different from the ones you use on a regular basis. Whether you're answering the phone, speaking with a client or brainstorming with a co-worker or supervisor. They aren't secret words that hypnotists are handed when they achieve a particular degree. It is not necessary to be a great master to use them. They aren't reserved for a select few who have spent years studying them and are now able to speak them fluently. Nope. They're at your disposal to get whatever you want!

What makes them power words isn't necessarily the words themselves, but the *way* in which they're used. Yep, that's really the secret behind making them 'hypnotic'. What do hypnotic power words do?

- They stimulate someone's imagination.
- They distract someone, putting their guards down.
- They weave pictures in the mind of the listener and their rationale is lowered.
- They activate senses and create associations.
- They link two things or ideas that wouldn't normally go together: for example, the words 'high risk' with 'pleasure' or 'benefits'.

What Are Ways You Use Hypnotic Language to Get What You Want?

- **Stop using pushy language, first and foremost.** Truly persuasive people understand their power and use it sparingly and knowingly. They understand that most conversations do not require trying to get someone to do or accept something. Aggressive pushers are a turn-off and will put most people on the defensive. When someone aggressively advocates a concept, especially when they do so with power and tenacity, it is the person who rarely questions or disagrees who finally receives consideration. Simply stated, they choose their battles carefully. Do you want to influence more people? Less frequently should you argue and advocate.
- **Try to do something for them before trying to convince them.** As a kid, you probably said something nice to your parents before asking them for something, right? Kids are smart!

    You can do this before you even pitch anything. If you start off a networking relationship with a favour, that person will be more likely to work with you later on. If you're going to talk to your boss for a promotion, bring him his favourite snack during the break and casually say, 'Hi! I saw this and thought you might be craving it!' You've broken their guard down, already.
- **Use the hypnotic hyperbole.** Details confuse you, and it takes work to provide them. So, don't. Instead, find grandiose words to describe your thinking. 'It's the greatest project ever' or 'I'm going to turn this company into a profit robot!' Generalizing enhances the glittering effect, too. 'Everyone knows how important this is' or 'All around the world, people

are realizing the value of the kind of services we provide.'
- **The language of giving and taking.** Make people feel indebted (subtly) so that they give you more and more, as and when you ask them to. Use the language of subtle giving and taking.

- Make the favour seem 'special': 'This is just for you, don't tell anyone else!' (and then do the exact same with anyone else at work.)
- Make the favour seem costly: 'It took me 3 days of 12-hours work a day. But I knew you needed it. I'm glad I could help!' (and maybe it took him just one day)
- Remind them of an old favour you've done for them subtly: 'It's a lot like when you needed $250 and I came from office, met you up and gave you cash, remember? I empathize with your situation now. I need the money so badly!' (by subtly reminding someone you were there for them when they needed you, you make them feel guilty for not doing the same.)

- **If you're leading the group, always use 'we'.** A group of selfless followers who identify with their teams is a leader's dream. Selfless individuals who identify with the team will readily die for that team—and for the leader—which empowers the leader while disempowering the individuals—too bad! Hence, much of a leader's manipulation seeks to influence people into investing more and more into the group, including emotional and identity-based investment. Master charmers leading a group tap into the member's hunger of wanting to belong in a tribe and work together for them, ultimately.

- The 'We' and 'Us' Talk: Seek to instil a culture of 'We' as part of your group-identity strategy and create a loyal army.
- Talk Up the Group: After all, you want the individuals to see the group as the solution to all of their problems.
- Make Up Enemies: This is classic in-group/out-group manipulation that our beloved politicians play against us. It's always 'us' versus 'them'. Make up an enemy, and people naturally become more cohesive—this enemy could be a rival team, a rival company, a rival leader…anything.
- Make the Individuals Dependent: Mind-masters don't want to fix the individuals for good but want them dependent on the group and on the leader. Keep them coming back for more.

- **Use their names when you address them.** 'You' is a placeholder for your name. Your name. I'm willing to bet you have no idea just how hypnotic your name actually is.

    Don't you automatically want to like people who have the same name as you? Don't you feel like they deserve more of a chance than other people? Many email marketers have latched onto the fact that a person's name is powerful—you probably receive emails with subject lines like, 'Jessy, top 10 copywriting tricks.' And many emails you get will start with your first name; long ones will include it several times. A person's name is so powerful that you have to have a very light touch when you use it.
- **'You, you and you!'** The word 'you' is magical. You don't have to be heavy-handed when using it in conversation because it's natural. Nonetheless, it encapsulates the same core self-obsession that gives your own name such force.

(Please understand that I am not criticizing you. We're all enamoured with ourselves. It's just part of the human condition.)

As a result, we get lulled when people talk about ourselves. What they're saying ignores the key aspect, leaving only the unconscious mind to be stimulated. What's more, guess what? Nothing excites us more than our own passions, aspirations, ambitions, objectives, yearnings, and emotions. That is all we have for the rest of our life. So long as your text addresses those concerns for your prospect, it will keep them engrossed in a semi-torpid state of contemplation.

- **'Imagine.'** Using the word imagine is a great way to lull people into doing what *you* want them to do, because it helps the person being hypnotized relax their rigid thinking patterns. When people are asked to engage their imaginations, they are more likely to imagine scenarios and possibilities that they would not have considered otherwise.

  'Imagine yourself feeling fully at ease as you stroll into a dinner party,' for example. Because they realize they're merely faking, a socially anxious person may be able to embody the sense of being relaxed in a social situation more easily when asked to do this. Once they know what the sensation feels like, they want more and more of it… and what do they do? They listen to you.

- **'Because…'** Using the word 'because' satisfies the brain's natural search for reasons. Because it's simply not important enough to dedicate brainpower to analysing the explanation, you can actually short-circuit the process and deceive the mind into going to the next stage of the sequence as if a valid reason had been given for modest requests. Give a good reason and 'you're in', so to speak.

- **Mix facts with fiction.** Your main task as a mind-control…I mean *persuader*, is to put the listener into an illusory environment so that you won't notice the manipulation but perceive it as a set of circumstances. Pepper in a few facts and figures while trying to persuade someone to do something to achieve success, and they will follow almost blindly.
- **It's *all* about the future.** Using future tense is a great way to establish confidence. It shows the other person that you are taking action and are ready to follow through on your promises. You may simply accomplish this by exploiting the term 'will'. 'We will' and 'Then we'll do this' are phrases that will help the person get used to the concept that something will happen. Again, don't be obnoxious. Instead of making decisions for the other person, talk about the possibilities and the consequences of those decisions.
- **'Remember.'** It gets people to go back into their mind, reduces resistance, because I am not asking you to do anything new, I am asking you to remember. You go back to the place where ideally you have been more resourceful where you can go into an emotional state that ideally the gain is positive.

    To use 'remember' more powerfully, take someone back to a positive moment. It takes them back and again; the unconscious mind can't tell between what's really happening up here and it becomes a mental rehearsal again. People are repeating that behaviour and therefore, they are more likely to repeat that behaviour. Now, they've done it in their mind. Isn't this great?

    Example: you want someone to partake with you in a new project involving a high risk. What do you say? 'Clara, remember how good we did the last time? Our profits may not have been perfect, but didn't we have a wonderful time where we learnt so much about innovation and the market trends?'

- **'What would it be like when…'** The power phrase what's it like when again capitalizes on the mind's desire to answer questions and fill in the blanks. So, if someone wanted hypnosis for success, the hypnotist may inquire, 'What does it feel like when you're absolutely successful?' The person who is being hypnotized will automatically embody the experience of having answered the question correctly.
- **Avoid weak words.** The way you phrase what you say matters as much or more than the actual content of it. If you are trying to sound convincing, this means avoiding saying things like:

> - 'Well, um…'
> - 'I think that maybe I…'
> - 'This might be the case…'
> - 'I mean…I guess…'
> - 'I don't really know.'
> - 'If I were —, then I could perhaps…'

- **Regulate your tone.** Ever heard the saying 'bewitching voice'? Some people get the gift of a voice that would make anybody do anything, just like a spell. Most hypnotists are given this gift, but they have to work to hone it. Forget about constricting your voice and speaking quickly; your main concern should be to enunciate, speak slowly, soften your tone, smile and seem confident. You can modify the meaning or tone of a sentence by emphasising key words. For instance, here is an example with the phrase, 'What do you think we can do about it?'

- Say it defensively (emphasizing the words 'would you'): 'What would you like us to do about it?'
- Say it with curiosity (emphasizing the words 'like us'): 'What would you like us to do about it?'
- Say it with apathy (not emphasizing any of the words): 'What would you like us to do about it?'

All of them create different meanings depending on your tone and emphasis. If you're targeting a particular person, always lower your tone during *'what would you'* and say these words slower and clearer. Works wonders!

- **Couple words with gestures.** Moving your hands and making facial expressions while you speak can make you seem confident and convincing. For instance, when you say something positive, smile a bit and open your eyes a little wider. If you don't move at all while you are speaking, people might become suspicious. On the other hand, it is important to not overdo it.

    For instance: you can laugh a little if you say something funny, but don't slap the table and act like it's the most hilarious thing you've ever heard.

    Likewise, if you are trying to convince your boss to extend your deadline, don't start breaking down and crying. Instead, calmly present them with real reasons that you think you need more time to give your absolute best and achieve success.

    If you're making someone imagine something while

trying to convince them, widen your eyes, show your palms, utter words in a soft, breathy voice and come a little closer to them for impact.

- **Sit right next to them.** Especially if they're in a bad mood, which most people at work usually are. It turns out that, psychologically, it's a lot easier to unload your anger on someone physically distant from you. It's just awkward to turn to someone immediately next to you and bawl that person out. So, if you sense steam coming from your boss's (or partner's) ears before a meeting, take control of the situation and sit right next to him. Your proximity will help keep the anger at bay.
- **Make them say 'no' before they say 'yes'.** In some situations, it's better to make an unrealistically large request first. The other party will say no (and feel a bad about it). That way, when you make your real request, he or she will feel obliged to say yes.
- **The lulling language of logic.** People are *easily* persuaded by logic. When someone is convinced to do something, they do it because they believe it is the correct or best course of action. Let's imagine you're trying to persuade a co-worker to take on one of the more difficult parts of an assignment you're both working on. Your teammate may object at first, but you can use logic to explain that he or she is more qualified to handle that area, which means the task will be completed faster and more efficiently, making both of you look good and helping the company in the process; this will also feed into their need for validation as you just acknowledged their expertise.
- **Don't sound like a tech-robot who is dead inside.** Don't be afraid to speak simply. More than technical words, what

matters is using vivid, simple and crisp words.

Remember that your goal is to seem clear and convincing, and to tap into people's weaknesses and emotions. If your audience doesn't understand what you are saying, it might seem that you are hiding something or don't really have anything to say. The more authentic you sound, the earlier you gain trust and convince someone to do something for you.

- When it's not acceptable, don't employ lofty words. If you can say 'improve' instead of 'ameliorate', for example, consider doing so.
- If you use technical terminology like 'synergy', ensure they are ones that your audience understands and utilizes.
- Make sure your audience understands what you mean if you use slang or informal language.

- **Sprinkle the sweet sugar of flattery, just a tad bit.** It's one of the cheaper tricks on this list, so be aware that a good percentage of the population will catch onto you quickly if you're too blunt or obvious. Rather than outright flattering your intended subject, utilize subtle language and off-the-cuff remarks to charm them. Instead of asking your boss, 'Hey, that's a pretty good suit, do you think I could take a day off tomorrow?' say, for example, 'I was wondering if I could take a day off tomorrow. I know you're typically accommodating and understanding, but I just wanted to make sure.'

Here's a great example of the words coming out of a master persuader's mouth:

> '**The more I think** about this upcoming project, **the more convinced I am** that **you** would perform **terrific** in it. **Imagine** the admiration you'll get everywhere **you** go, **how amazing you'll feel** every time **you** are congratulated by someone for your successes. And **as you think** about the **thrill** of leading this project, **you find yourself wishing** you give your best, because you know **you deserve a chance** to show your real talent. **Sooner or later,** you have to see the leader within **you, which means** that this project is your *ideal* opportunity and **it's now or never. Just pretend** for a minute that **you** *already are* leading it, and **you'll realize** just how **perfect** it is for **you**, your passions and your personality. **It's as if** this project was designed just for **you!**'

Five Takeaways for You to Skim Over:

- Office politics isn't a nightmare when you use them to your advantage and get what you want.
- Know who's powerful in your office and have your eyes on them—charm them first, and you've charmed 90 per cent of the workforce.
- Do not trust others with personal opinions or complaints. Anything you say in the office can be used against you.
- Have your foot in each circle. Don't piss one group off to impress the other—always create a middle ground. Remember, the nice guy has to be loved by *everyone* in the office.
- Use hypnotic language to conjure images and ideas in others' heads and get them to say 'yes' *every single time (*without even having to ask!*)*

9

THE CUNNING ONE CLIMBS THE CORPORATE LADDER

People don't get promoted for doing their jobs really well. They get promoted by demonstrating their potential to do more.[27]

—Tara Jaye Frank, Founder and CEO of TJF Career Modeling LLC.

I considered myself an ambitious person when I started my career, yet I listened to what everyone said about having to put in my time. Rack up some points. Earn my stripes. Problem is, this method takes time. Years, possibly even decades. Even though this is what I was trained to expect, I never felt like I had time for that. I've always been a fast learner, and I wanted to test my limits—not bide my time and wait for someone else to decide if and when I was ready to move up the ladder.

You've made it! You've spent countless nights burying your nose in homework, class notes, and tutorials, as well as a

---

[27]Tara Jaye Frank, *Say Yes: A Woman's Guide to Advancing Her Professional Purpose*, Gold House Press, 2015.

significant amount of time job hunting. You've completed your education and secured employment. So, what's next? This is the start of a new chapter for some of you. Whether it's a specific project, role or company, you've set yourself stretch goals and you're eager to fast track your career to achieve your desired level of success. But the path to career success is a darn difficult climb, riddled with obstacles and hurdles around every bend. In fact, most successes are slow, challenging and do not happen overnight. Nevertheless, there are measures that you can take to equip yourself for this ascent and move your career into the fast lane—being slow is so twentieth century.

Many of us were probably raised to believe that our hard work should 'speak for itself'. Unfortunately, when it comes to getting a promotion, that might not be enough. While 'climbers' on the corporate ladder have a bad connotation, the truth is that there's nothing wrong with wanting to be recognized for your accomplishments. It's always these climbers who are the modern alpha employees.

A promotion is an exciting thing. You take on additional duties, advance to the next level in your job, gain a greater sense of accomplishment and earn more money. However, getting promoted necessitates more than just doing a good job. Even if you are a top performer who takes initiative and achieves your objectives, you may still need to persuade your boss that you are deserving of a promotion. This begins with a dialogue and a persuasive argument for what you want and why you deserve it.

Being a valuable member of the organization is a key first step if you want a better title or a higher income in the future. But if you really want to stand out as a future leader, here are several steps you can take to learn how to get promoted at work.

Firstly, let me tell you your hard work isn't half as important as you working smartly is. Your dad or granddad must have told you, if you want to be successful in the long run, you have to put long hours into work. You have to start early, before everyone else, and you have to stay up late when everyone else is already enjoying their afternoons and evenings.

Now, I don't agree with that one single bit. If this was the trick, why are so many people working hard but only a few becoming successful? That's because smart work is what makes the difference.

Work (in the traditional sense) brings to mind long hours chained to the desk, overtime and scheduled breaks. Success comes from putting in the hours; the old adage, 'Work hard and you'll see the results,' is a popular one, but the results aren't always there to back it up. We've all been in that situation. You've been working hard for hours and are thinking to yourself, 'What did I actually accomplish today? I'm fatigued, I haven't moved in a long time, and I still have a lengthy list of things to accomplish.' Perhaps the quality of your work isn't that great. You start to get annoyed with yourself. 'Why haven't I gotten that promotion? Why do I never get what I want?'

Smart work is *all* about contacts and networking, essentially achieving more in less time, organizing priorities to enable you to use your time well. 'We all have the same amount of time each and every single day. What we do with that time is entirely up to us.'

Let me tell you what your parents or teachers never would—hard work is extremely overrated and outdated! I see this especially with young professionals who've just finished college and brag about the number of hours they make 'on the job'. In our society, we have this illness of thinking that we all have to work our tails off to achieve something that only 1 per cent of the population achieves. What irritates me even more is how hard effort is equated with putting in the maximum number of hours.

Allow me to give you an example. Many of my classmates studied for weeks for an exam throughout my studies. I generally arrived up a week before the exam, making sure I thoroughly looked through earlier examinations and devoted 80 per cent of my effort on 20 per cent of the most important study material. This way, I effortlessly passed exams leaving others frustrated and thinking I must have cheated or something. The fact is that I worked really hard in the final week before an exam, to the point where others mocked me as the 'Last-5-Seconds-Guy'. But I put the quality of time invested over its quantity. Even until this day, I rather sleep in, work out in the morning, enjoy a damn good breakfast before trying to be as productive as possible for the remaining hours instead of spending my whole day at the office. Especially entrepreneurs being very passionate about their projects, they seem to mistakenly think that if they put twice the number of hours, they'll have twice the amount of chance for success. The only thing they will be successful in is getting a burn-out, failed relationships and an unhealthy lifestyle.

Bosses won't promote you for working hard. What bosses are looking for are people who create new openings and new opportunities for the company. In other words, they're looking for *smart* people. Working hard is a thing of the 1980s. The secret to success is to make wise career and task decisions in order to raise your profile. You are not working intelligently if you spend all of your waking hours at your job. Knowing what jobs you excel at and delegating the others is the key to working smarter. Instead of being fatigued by repetitive activities, working smarter means fuelling oneself with creativity and motivation.

Above all, working smart entails self-reflection and streamlining your workflow procedures in order to maximize productivity. You demonstrate leadership by working smarter.

How Does Working Too Hard Turn You into a Weakling?

- This one's the first one that comes to our minds—your productivity and creativity get stalled. Let's face it, the more you work, the more stressed you become and the more likely you are to become less productive. Despite putting in the hours, if you are burnt-out, it takes longer to complete a task, which can become a vicious cycle.
- You kick yourself after the fact for not speaking up in a meeting. You only come to realize your point of view on something after the discussion is over.
- You hate your colleagues for getting all the benefits of *you* working for them whereas you remain invisible.
- You feel overwhelmed and pulled in multiple directions especially as emails and requests for work or input come in.
- Your calendar is full with back-to-back meetings and no time to focus on yourself or critical priorities. You basically have no life.
- You take on others' tasks and get paid nothing for that. It's not a good sign if your job feels like a high school group project—where you suddenly find yourself doing all the work while other people slack off. You're the person that everyone goes to at the last minute when they need something done because they know you will sacrifice your time, energy and other plans to get it done.
- If you need 80+ hours a week to finish your tasks, this might send off the wrong signal to your bosses. They may

see this as an indication that you are overwhelmed by your work, that you are unable to complete your chores in a reasonable period of time, and that you are not ready to take on further responsibilities.
- Do you feel like you're constantly working so hard to prove yourself, but you never get any recognition for it? It might be the case that you're always trying to do more to please or 'prove yourself' to others at work, but you feel like you're a 'sucker' at work and no one respects you or your time. You might even see co-workers you started with being awarded and promoted ahead of you.

What Are Some Ways You Gush into the Sea of Promotions (Without Ripping Your Hair Apart)?

- **Have a plan (as clichéd as that sounds!)** Do you know what your goals are? If not, you must take some time to identify them. Only once you precisely know what your goals are will you be able to see what it takes to get there. Smart people always know what they want; they're not slow, confused or dazed. Ask yourself these questions:

> - Where am I now?
> - What were my highlights from the past year?
> - What are my core strengths? How can I flaunt them more?
> - How can I improve upon my weaknesses and make this work visible?
> - Where do I want to be a year from now?
> - Where does my boss think I could be in a year?

Set milestones and deadlines to drive you to complete your tasks rather than becoming overwhelmed by the scale of your ambitions. Break down large goals into smaller components if required.

If you want to be a professional musician, for example, you should make a plan to achieve that objective. This is what it might look like:

- Enrol in a professional music course full-time.
- Learn everything you can about music and the instrument you want to play.
- You've dedicated a significant portion of your free time to practising your chosen instrument.
- Work with others to improve your abilities and confidence.
- Look for ways to set yourself apart from the pack in terms of your playing, look, and personality.
- Keep in mind that your strategy is an important part of your success, as it allows you to think forward and keep track of your accomplishments.

- **Know what your beloved leader is into.** If your boss likes having you around, he's going to keep you around. One trick is to notice his interests and be a sport, always! Your boss might say, 'I'm going to see Deadpool this weekend.' A stupid employee who isn't thinking will say, 'I hate that film! X-Men films are so much better!' But a smarter alpha employee would instead say, 'Hey, stay after the end credits start rolling! I've heard there are hints for the next Spiderman film!' or maybe 'Isn't Ryan Reynolds hilarious? Gotta love that guy!'

- **Be proactive.** If you're the type of person to simply sit at your desk, do your job and not get involved with the inner workings of the office, you're not likely to go very far. The inevitable truth is that you have to be assertive. Suggest new ideas and try new things. Take initiative. Even if your idea fails, your leaders will still be impressed that you had the courage to try something new. That way, you most definitely outshine the weaklings of the office.
- **Work Hard and Smart.** Go above and beyond at work, doing more than the minimal requirements. Work harder than others on your team (especially when your boss is watching), but also work smarter. Volunteer for high-visibility projects. Seek to contribute more, and make yourself the go-to person. If your instinct is to jump on everything, you'll seem desperate and spread yourself thin. 'If you say yes too much, your performance will drop,' says Larry Myler, business strategist and author of *Indispensable by Monday: Learn the Profit-Producing Behaviors That Will Help Your Company and Yourself*. 'If you say no, you don't look like a team player.'[28] Find out what opportunities are most profitable—and visible—for the company and snag those. If you're overwhelmed, ask about priorities. Then, suggest how to delegate what's on your plate.
- **You are more than your job description.** Your job description might be limited but that doesn't limit you. Do whatever is assigned to you, then ask what else you can do, even if it's in another department or on another project. Help wherever you can, whenever you can, however

---

[28] Larry Myler, *Indispensable By Monday: Learn the Profit-Producing Behaviors that will Help Your Company and Yourself*, Wiley, 2010.

you can—the smart player is a champ in every department and he knows how to charm the entire office, not just his/her team.

- **Become indispensable.** Whether it's inventing a new program that will save your firm money or becoming a client's go-to person, put your boss in a position where he can't afford to lose you. Document your successes. 'If you're only on email, no one knows what your client contact is like,' Mark Jeffries, author of *The Art of Business Seduction: A 30-Day Plan to Get Noticed, Get Promoted and Get Ahead*, says. 'You want to be visible by racing out because you have lunch with a client or vocal by talking on the phone. The trick is to get people to come to the conclusion that you are successful without bragging.'[29] Employ these strategies to secure a strong foothold in this shaky economy. When the opportunities for getting promoted start to solidify, you could be the first in line to move up.

- **Behave like your superiors.** Do you know the advice to act 'as if'? If you want to a job farther up the career ladder, act 'as if' you already have that job. Consider yourself to be a higher-ranking official. Pay attention to how individuals in positions above you manage, delegate, coach, and communicate, and model their actions after them. What abilities have they honed? Acquire those abilities.

- **Or at times, make them obsolete.** It's ironic, but the best way to get promoted is to make your boss' job easier. And the best way to do that is to make his or her job obsolete. You're not really putting your manager out of a job—you're

---

[29] Mark Jeffries, *The Art of Business Seduction: A 30-Day Plan to Get Noticed, Get Promoted and Get Ahead*, John Wiley & Sons, 2010.

allowing him or her to trust your work. In turn, he or she can focus on new areas that the higher-ups have needed to address for some time. Strong work goes up the chain, improves the company and gets you noticed.

- **Under-promise and surprise them.** If you want to impress people, well, impress them already. But *how*?

   Simple—exceed their expectations! The single biggest factor in accelerating my career was my ability to impress my clients, colleagues, managers and executives. (Just be warned: this is a tactic only to be used if you can back it up. Over-promising and under-delivering will set you back eons.) If your goal is to always do more than what you signed up to do, two things will happen. First, everyone will start expecting great things from you. Second, someone's going to notice your talents aren't being properly utilized, and you'll find your way into a new job title. If it's not someone at your current job, it will be someone you network or interview with.

- **Be a gold mine.** Be more than that nerdy person at that desk! Continuously strive to up-skill yourself and learn new skills. Take certification courses. Study and follow all the industry leaders wherever they are active and attend conferences. The more you learn and know, the more of an asset you will be to your employer.

- **Get those projects in your arsenal.** Companies place a premium on employees who know how to deliver. If you can prove that you can consistently own projects from start to finish, you will not only get promoted, but you'll also make yourself indispensable.

- **Know your superior's schedule inside out.** Does your leader tend to leave work at the same time each day? Or does he like to stroll by your section of the office at a certain hour in the afternoon? Whenever he's most likely to swing by your desk, that's when you should be scheduling your client calls—or whatever other activity will make you look *most productive*. Whether or not you're busting your butt the rest of the day, your boss will only believe what he sees.

- **Promote smart, not shamelessly.** There is a thin line between evidence-based smart self-promotion versus open, desperate self-promotion. Instead of saying, 'I deserve this because I'm a high performer, like other people who have received a promotion in the past year,' say 'I would like to review my performance over the past year with you and provide you with some examples of how I've taken the initiative to support the collective goals of the team/division/business.' Stick to the facts you've documented that reflect your track record, and provide vivid examples of incidents that showcase your outstanding performance.
- **Donate to your boss' cause if you can.** Charity brings you higher profits—yes, I said it, shelling out a little time or money will, in turn, get you more cash and power.

  This may seem like a super-obvious way to win the head honcho's favour. And it is. But that doesn't mean it won't work! If your company's chief is promoting some organization, you bet he'll notice—and appreciate—you donating time or money to his cause.
- **Play well with others.** Besides working on tasks, work on your relationships and work smart. This means charming your co-workers all day, every day.

  Yes, your co-workers, in one respect, are your competition, and many of them are ruthless about their advancement. Nonetheless, you have to demonstrate an ability to work with people you don't necessarily like or want to collaborate with. If a big deadline is approaching and your co-worker seems to be falling behind, offer to help. You know the adage: keep your friends close, and your enemies closer. The more you work with your competition, the more you'll know them. Most importantly, while you're gathering valuable information about your competition's work habits, your bosses will realize how helpful you are to your co-workers (and how well-suited you are for an even better position).

Once you win over your peers, you will find others lifting you up on their own—they are rooting for you! You'll also find it easier to influence them and have your way without bruising their egos.

- **Sometimes, just straight up ask for one, maybe?** Don't be afraid to tell your boss that you *want* a promotion. They can assist you in developing core talents and keep you in mind for future promotions. You don't have to demand a promotion to start the dialogue. Instead, once you've complimented them and made some small conversation, ask them what it will take to get one. This will put your boss in the position of a guide or a mentor, and get them equally invested in your career's success.
- **Maintain a small 'brag' folder.** Surpassed your goal for the second time in a row? Cracked a big account? Make a note every time you accomplish something, and add it to your brag folder. This includes any time you get a shout-out or a thank-you from a co-worker or a client. Include any real statistics or metrics that back up your accomplishments as well.
- **Outmanoeuvre your competitors (I meant co-workers!)**

1) **Lend a hand**. 'It sounds counterintuitive,' says leadership coach Ray White, 'but helping your co-workers and giving them credit is a great way to outmanoeuvre them... Supervisors and peers want to work with people who get things done, who don't steal credit, who are willing to lend a helping hand, and who are overall leaders.'[30]
2) **Train the newbies.** Nobody wants to waste time on half-baked potatoes with no power, right? Wrong. Improving new workers around you will put you in a better position since you're helping your boss solve one of their greatest problems—wasting time and energy on half-baked potatoes. That way, you also charm the naïve newbies into rooting for you. And these newbies are the future of the firm.
3) **Take the lead.** One of the best ways to outmanoeuvre your co-workers is to achieve a leadership position on a project—especially if it advances your boss' agenda.
4) **Stay mum about your own agendas and modus operandi.** Don't tell your co-workers when, where and how you plan on networking with powerful leaders or talking to your boss about the promotion. Just don't.
5) **Speak up.** If you notice that a certain colleague is trying to outsmart you, stealing your ideas and suggesting them in team meetings, speak up about it. You could say something like: 'Thank you for sharing the idea that I mentioned earlier, Jared. I think it will be...' and then continue to elaborate on your thought process behind it.
6) **Kiss up to your boss a little bit.** Tell everyone how great

---

[30]Ray White, *Connecting Happiness and Success: Guide to Creating Success Through Happiness: 1*, Xilo Media, 2014.

your superior is, or how much you admire his leadership. 'Trust me, he will hear about it and appreciate the evangelism,' says Roy Cohen, a career coach and author of *The Wall Street Professional's Survival Guide*. 'On the other hand, kissing his ass in person could make you look like a suck-up, which could hurt you,' Cohen adds.[31]

7) **Know what's cooking,** from a safe distance. Water cooler chitchat about how Hugh from Accounting hooked up with the receptionist isn't a classy way to spend a large chunk of time, but there can be some valuable nuggets of information hidden under all that talk. It's important to learn not only the reputations of your co-workers but the stories going around about you. If you have a reputation of being late for work or staying up all night drinking with the guys, you're less likely to be seen by the higher-ups as a reliable employee who is ready for some more power. Additionally, office gossip also has some positive aspects—you'll know when a job is opening up before it's announced, how to get on the inside track with some of your bosses and maybe even the kind of person they're looking to hire.

8) **Know the powerful better than your co-workers do.** The moral is that you need to build personal relationships with your superiors. Remember their birthdays, ask about their kids, and offer to buy them a drink after work once in a while. Attend every meeting they'll allow you to sit in on, and offer to help with any extra projects around the office. If your company offers a mentoring or shadowing program,

---

[31] Roy Cohen, *The Wall Street Professional's Survival Guide: Success Secrets of a Career Coach*, Financial Times/ Prentice Hall, 2010.

take full advantage of it! If you want to get to know your bosses and learn how they run the company, there's no better way to learn than to watch them first-hand. You already know office politics is a dirty game to play, but it's often necessary in the business jungle.

9) **Win even if you don't.** What do I mean when I say this? Just in case you lose your promotion to a co-worker, make the most out of their power. Consider how the advancement of a co-worker can help you.

   Remember all the things you and your co-worker used to talk about when you were in the same cubicle? Perhaps you thought a department policy was inefficient or that staff should be allowed to work from home more frequently. What's more, guess what? Your co-worker might be able to make those adjustments now that he or she is in a position of authority. I remember telling a co-worker that I hadn't heard from Olivia, our chief marketing officer, in a long time. 'I have a one-on-one meeting with Olivia today; do you want me to get you some time on her calendar?' remarked that co-worker when she became my manager. Finally, I had a direct line of communication with the CMO.

   Remember that your co-worker has been in your shoes before—symbolically, of course—she knows what you want and is now in a position to make it happen. Instead of dying of envy, make use of it.

- **Respond on time.** Yes, yes, I know I said mystery was great, but that doesn't mean you become invisible. Don't be the annoying employee who is always 'too busy' to answer emails, take calls, reply to IMs, etc. You don't want to be branded as unresponsive and rigid, as this could jeopardize your chances of advancement. If you want to rise to the top, constantly be responsive and don't make up ridiculous excuses for not responding to individuals, especially if they are powerful. While no one wants you to be a 'yes guy' or a 'dogsbody', if a request exposes you to a new part of the company or allows you to build a new skill set that will help you advance faster, take advantage of it.

- **Network, enough said.** No one wants to hear networking is a part of the plan, but we all know it can't be ignored. It's like brushing your teeth. You might be tired and your bed is calling, but you know you'll regret it if you don't brush. Networking is pretty much like that. If you're not making waves where you're at, branching out to your network is the best way to get a feel for what you should do next. The beauty of a good network is that these people are usually objective and often have your best interests at heart. If they think you can do better somewhere else, they'll tell you.

This is great, not only for the ego boost if you're undervalued but the sanity check that you do deserve more than what you're getting. Your network has been there, done that and they'll spill all their secrets if you're lucky. Tap into this resource early and often, and you'll have a perpetual career counsellor at your fingertips.

Here Are Some Things You Don't Do to Get That Promotion

- **Wrong place and time.** Make sure the venue is suitable for the discussion and that you've scheduled it in advance, with enough time allotted. Avoid pre-lunch and end of day—but be flexible; the time of day may be helpful, but if your boss has had a major setback or horrendously busy day, better to wait.

- **Privacy is a myth.** Cubicles are easy to look in on and listen in on. Computers are also easy to look in on (and also because they are the legal property of the firm). Don't write or view anything that could endanger your position and your promotability. Keystroke monitors and other digital 'security' tools are easy to install and cheap. Phone monitors, too. You are at work to work. Don't give your competitors *anything* that they can use against you. Use your cell phone for personal email on your own time. This means you are using your own phone provider and not the Wi-Fi of your company.
- **Don't act like a god.** Sure, you want to be noticed, but it's important not to come across as arrogant. Do your best to show that you're confident, not cocky. The nice guy always acts humble, remember?
- **Don't bring others up, please.** There are other people in your department who did less and still got promoted (at least, in your opinion). So, you are going to bring that up in the conversation, right?

  Wrong! Doing that comes across as trashing your colleagues and perhaps your boss as well—who likely made the decision to give your colleague the promotion. The nice guy always remains in everyone's good books.
- **Don't be a wallflower.** If key decision makers and power holders don't know you, you are not likely to wind-up on a promotion list; it's pretty logical.

  Office wallflowers can usually be found eating lunch at their desks, working alone at their computers, sitting quietly in meetings and avoiding all social contact. If this

describes you and you want to be promoted, then you need to get out more.
- **Don't forget to create a case.** Know the skills the position you're aiming for requires. Make sure you're prepared to demonstrate how your skills and accomplishments are a good match for the job. I mean, your immediate boss might love you. But they need to justify the decision to promote you to their boss and finance. And their boss and finance don't give a darn about your oh-so-strong personal relationship.

  So, to act like you really care about your boss, make it easy for them. Present them the business case, so they are ready when asked to defend your promotion. Once you do half of their job for them, they're more tempted, more impressed and more convinced.
- **Don't whine.** How often are you in your boss's office complaining about unfair policies, difficult co-workers or unpleasant working conditions? If the answer is 'frequently', then you are probably viewed as a high maintenance employee. And your boss has probably shared this opinion with other managers. Remember, you're an employee, not a beautiful mistress. Your complaining makes you annoying.
- **Don't beg!** This one's literally the premise of this book. We are not beggars; we are clever go-getters. You may have childcare to pay for or a sick family member, but that isn't a good reason for your company to spend more money on you. Avoid using your personal life to beg for a promotion. Subtly, smartly, sell yourself instead. How, you may ask?

  Show them you've earned a promotion—start by keeping something of an inventory of your accomplishments. If you land a new account, record it. If you revise a proposal in a way that helps resolve a stubborn problem, write that down, too. This will help you get a better handle on your contributions. Then, when you have occasion to mention these accomplishments to your boss or manager, do so. If something comes up in passing, let them know that you 'enjoyed being involved' and that you were 'excited' about your 'contribution'. You might also bring your list to your next performance review or negotiation meeting. You can't get promoted until relevant parties understand the weight and significance of your contribution to the company in your current position. So, be sure to let them know, *cleverly*.

- **Lastly, just don't outshine the master. Ever.** 'Being defeated is hateful, and besting one's boss is either foolish or fatal. Most people do not mind being surpassed in good fortune, character, or temperament, but no one…likes to be surpassed in intelligence.'[32] says writer and philosopher Baltasar Gracián, and *he's spot on*.

If you are more intelligent than your master, seem the opposite—make *him* appear more intelligent. Show you're there seeking help—acting naive and make it seem you need his expertise by feigning ignorance. Don't contradict or embarrass your boss in front of others. When you disagree or point out a problem, do it privately and with respect. Begin with something like, 'As per my knowledge….' or 'I was doing some research on this topic, and I found out that….do you think *this* could be the case?' The master mind-controller knows well to never try to one-up his master, openly.

---

[32] Baltasar Gracian, *The Art of Worldly Wisdom: A Pocket Oracle*, Currency, 1991.

Five Takeaways for You to Skim Over:

- If you keep slaving away beyond work hours to bag that promotion, I have bad news for you: it's not going to work!
- You have to work smart along with working hard—climbing the corporate ladder has a lot to do with your contacts and networks.
- To get promoted, always remain in the good books of all your superiors—show you are irreplaceable by acquiring new skills, acting all selfless with team members and taking the lead in projects.
- Target tasks and projects that are being monitored by the big bosses—that way, your hard work isn't going down the drain.
- Outshine your peers, but don't ever try to outshine your boss. Make his job easy but *do not* make him feel smaller to you. That's workplace suicide!

10

ACE YOUR ARGUMENTS

Persuasion is achieved by the speaker's personal character when the speech is so spoken as to make us think him credible. We believe good men more fully and more readily than others: this is true generally whatever the question is, and absolutely true where exact certainty is impossible and opinions are divided.

—Aristotle

When you get into an argument, you're clearly trying to get across a certain point. And if you're being totally honest, you'd probably love nothing more than to 'win' that fight and prove your conflict companion wrong.

Now, I could act like all of those self-help gurus, tell you to 'let it go, value your happiness and be the bigger guy' but I say, 'No, you *have* to win, *always.*'

Office argument is the most taboo word for some people—the weak ones, let's just say. Conflict is a pervasive thing at the workplace. A workplace disagreement, in its most basic form, is simply about the disparities between people at work; differences in beliefs, ambitions and conflicts of interests are frequently manifested as arguments. Everything boils down to human interactions and relationships. That is something that the corporate brain is well aware of.

There is no need to be afraid of office politics; the mind-controller knows he always gets his way somehow. Where there will be opinions, there will always be disagreements and the corporate jungle is notorious for that. For many people, arguing is something to avoid. But arguments can be used for good—they can help you gain the upper-edge over your workplace enemies, if handled tactfully.

Like physical fights, verbal fights can leave both sides bloodied. Even when you win, you end up not better off, unless you win with subtlety, class and smartness. If disputes were merely competitions, like tennis tournaments, your chances would be almost as bad. Pairs of opponents knock the ball back and forth until just one winner emerges from the field of competitors. Everyone else is a loser—who is the lone winner? You, after having read this chapter.

- **The impact of one alphabet: 'I'.** When you do argue with a colleague, deliver your points from the 'I' perspective. Rather than saying, 'You do this,' explain how the other person's behaviour makes you feel. Starting sentences with 'I feel pushed aside' or 'I'm upset because…' keeps you from casting blame on the other person, and will make it less likely for her to respond in a defensive manner.
- **Know your foe.** Sometimes, you won't know what your opponent values or what their background is—but sometimes, you will. Use that information. 'Most people are either reactive or analytical,' says Prince Ghuman, a professor at Hult International Business School and co-author of *Allure:*

The Neuroscience of Consumerism. 'Some people tend to be more reactive, so you can convince them using techniques that appeal to them—emotion and empathy,' he suggests. 'Others seem to be more deliberate—you'll need to provide an analytical support for your argument.'[33]

- **Kill them with kindness.** There are few better masters of manipulation than FBI negotiators. They are trained to defuse tight situations and persuade hostage takers and suicide jumpers to change their minds—or so it appears in the movies. Negotiators employ a five-stage method to modify their targets' behavioural intentions, and you may use the same strategy to your arguments.

1) **Active Listening**–Allow them to talk freely, nod, and make sounds or gestures of acknowledgement rather than instantly responding with your own attack. With nothing to fight back with, they'll be able to prolong the sting of their strike.
2) **Pretend to Empathize**–When you first respond, it's not to fight back but to show your appreciation (not the same as agreement) to their point of view.
3) **Build Trust**–You can now lead the talk towards common ground once the fire has died down and they don't regard you as an adversary. Build a sense of mutuality and trust by getting their buy-in on topics you both agree on.
4) **Influence**–Now you can gently encourage them towards your point of view.

---

[33]Eustacia Huen, 'How Neuroscience Explains Our Obsession With Food Mashups', *Forbes*, 30 August 2018, https://www.forbes.com/sites/eustaciahuen/2018/08/30/neurosciencefood/?sh=5b53da3a31fd, Accessed on 10 February 2022.

> **5) Change Their Mind**– Finally, having earned their trust and shifted their mind-set, you should be pushing at an open door to actually change their minds and get them to agree with you.

- **Rope-a-dope.** A simple but incredibly effective method of winning an argument is to simply give ground first on something meaningful but not critical. This lulls your opponent into a false sense of security, making them lower their mental guard and dial down their animosity level. And *that's* the moment you strike.

  Go further and make yourself look like an unworthy opponent by openly conceding their 'superior' knowledge and experience on the subject. Instinctively, your opponent will begin to pull their punches (since most people don't like to be considered bullies or pick on an inferior opponent). It's why a trained soldier is perplexed when confronted with a flower-wielding hippie. Then, once you've detected that they've mentally relaxed and switched off, pounce with your strongest points. They won't expect it, and you'll have a few moments to pound home your advantage before they psychologically tighten up again. It's a one-two punch. The classic 'Rope-a-Dope'. You win because they don't see you coming.

- **Don't show you're losing your cool.** Yelling, screaming, and losing control of your emotions during an argument instantly makes you seem subordinate to the person with whom you're in confrontation with—why? Because you're making them seem like the nice guy. You cannot let them snatch your persona from you.

You have already lost the battle if you lose your calm. Your arguments and position will carry more weight if you articulate them thoughtfully and reasonably. While it may be difficult to explain your point of view without getting emotional, try your hardest to keep tears and anger at bay.

- **'I could be wrong' makes you *always right*.** If you're in the discussion already, admit you could be wrong and you'll always emerge as the unofficial winner. Why?

- **You save face.** If you do turn out to be even partially wrong, you have saved face by already acknowledging the possibility.
- **They disarm.** It's easy to dig in and deny anything the other side has to say, but by admitting to possibly being wrong, you disarm the situation and show you're willing to listen.
- **They reciprocate.** Now that you've admitted the possibility of being wrong, the other side has room to safely do the same, as well as hear you out on your side. This is psychological: the minute you pretend to let your guard down, they'll put theirs down too.

- **Face interrogation, head on.** Avoiding questions in front of your co-workers does nothing but damage. If you want to convince them of your greatness, look at them and answer quickly—and do so without a smattering of 'ums', 'ahs' and 'likes' to prove your intelligence.

Answering quickly, calmly, without any evident signs of intentional delay and without looking away will help you to appear more intelligent, even if your response isn't the best or brightest. The worst thing you can do is to act like you didn't hear your name being called on.

- **Everyone loves tales.** Storytelling works hand-in-hand with empathy and puts data to support your argument in context. Pull all your information together—using empathy, facts and emotions—to create a compelling story and your argument will be tougher to beat. When your point seems part of a narrative arc, each aspect of what you're arguing is harder to pick on.
- **Play around with the aggressor.** If I have an opponent who's aggressive, *I love it*, because it's only a matter of time before you put a pin in him and he loses all his air. To be persuasive, it's much better to be horribly reasonable and as charming as possible. But even if you're really nice, you've always got to be in control.

  In court, I'd like the jurors to like me and trust that what I'm saying is genuine. It's important to pay attention to both your words and your body language. Everything you do is being watched by the jury. Jurors want to believe in you, so make sure they don't think you're just projecting your own personality and that what you're saying is true and relevant to the facts. If I have to be tough with one witness, I will make sure that they note how pleasant I am on other instances. So they believe the witness deserves it because, look at him now, he's quite pleasant.
- **Keep your chin up (even if you know you're wrong).** Now this one's real sneaky. Don't try it with your boss. When you're making your points, occasionally and gently use phrases like 'I'm pretty sure', 'I read somewhere that…' and 'That day, I heard…' If you don't sound 100 per cent sure of yourself, you give your opponent an opening to attack your argument. Even if you don't quite believe what you're saying, keep saying it like you're absolutely certain it's true.

You'll make your foe question his own beliefs.
- **A little exaggeration goes a *long* way.** 'So if all your friends jumped off a cliff, would you follow them and jump off as well?' I'm sure all of us have heard statements like this at some points of our lives.

  As tiring as these statements now are, they follow an age-old and still very effective approach of pushing an opponent's position to its logical extreme in order to highlight its inherent flaws.

  The real key once you've set out that exaggeration, however, is to then behave as though that extreme position is the actual argument your opponent is making. However hard they insist, don't let them revert back to their original more reasonable point where they are stronger. Keep the discussion focused on that extreme position, highlight how ridiculous it is and force them to try to justify it.

  If you're lucky, they'll get infuriated and as we know, *angry people always lose.*
- **Get handsy (not in that way!)** I'm not talking about flirting or throwing fists. Nope.

  However, body language is powerful, when used correctly. When used randomly and without intent, it can seem silly and totally useless; but if you plan on making a point and hope to convince your co-workers of it, consider using your flattened palm. Lay your palm flat against the desk or table and curl your fingertips downward if you want every point you make to be heard as a true and meaningful consideration. This gesture is meant to convey confidence, helping those around you to see that you mean business. There's no weak, waffling hand business here; just a firm, steady line of power.

- **And play footsy (again, no crazy ideas!)** Carefully, angle your feet whenever you're attempting to draw your co-worker or opponent in your direction and into your favour. In fact, the position of your feet can indicate who your allies are, where your allegiances lie and of course, who your enemies are.

  When someone's feet are slanted away from you, it means they don't want to engage with you; they're simply doing it to be polite. However, if their toes are oriented in your direction, they are extending outstretched arms to welcome you. Practise the same, and always point your feet towards your co-workers; those around you will think they're warmly welcomed. *Think.*
- **Stand up!** Take a pointer from a president, politician or professor: position yourself so you're slightly higher up than your opponent. If he's sitting down, stand up to create a sense of authority. It's a power move—you truly have the high ground.
- **Play with their heads a little.** Although you can't quite perform magic tricks in the middle of a meeting to convince your co-workers that you have the best, most viable ideas or reasoning. You can conduct a bit of a mind trick by implanting memories within your co-workers' heads. So, if you want to convince others that you're right or that your ideas are agreeable, remind them of the day during which you shared your genius idea over lunch, or the multiple meetings prior at which you proposed the exact same idea (even though you didn't). Give them a few suggestive details, and they'll quickly fill in the blanks in an effort to 'remember' your statements so they don't appear out of the know.
- **The object-barrier.** This is a sneaky trick but works like

wonders. Now remember, this one shouldn't be tried with a boss or any superior. Only with a co-worker when they're babbling about something you couldn't care less about.

Carry something in your hand when they're arguing with you, like a cell phone, pair of glasses or a pen. He'll feel like he doesn't have your full attention, and as a result, will become flustered.

- **The stare game.** Stare at their forehead just between and slightly above the eye-line while talking to someone. It throws them off their game and they have a harder time lying to you or trying to influence you.
- **Randomly insert a compliment.** Give someone a sincere compliment during an argument. If they are decent people, it will throw them off guard. They will then feel inclined to be more pliable.
- **Don't let your eyes wander.** If you want to appear more commanding and more intelligent, stop looking to the sky for all of your answers. Although it's incredibly tempting to gaze upward and roll your eyes away from your staring opponent(s), don't do it. When you're looking for solutions, turning upward comes across as a clumsy and useless move. If you look up at the ceiling, your co-workers will think you're looking for a solution everywhere you can find it. Instead, no matter how uncomfortable you are, establish their trust in you by making eye contact; this behaviour gives the impression that you are staring straight at them, even if you aren't.
- **Press the pause button.** Use silence to your advantage when negotiating. People have a natural tendency to be uncomfortable with silence and will often do whatever it takes to break it. Just be patient.

- **Create confusion.** Confusion clouds a person's logic and hence, is a bullet to their head during an argument. Confusion also frustrates, which is a bullet to the heart as the person gets all worked up and emotional.

1) **Steer into a different dimension.** Respond with a completely unrelated topic just as your opponent believes they've won. Give them a praise, send them a photo of your favourite plant, or say something entirely out of the blue like, 'I love poodles!' The individual with whom you're debating will most likely have no idea how to respond.

    Perhaps you're having a heated argument with a co-worker. Respond to shake things up saying, 'Also, off-topic but, I adore the colour of your sweater!'

2. **Use long, complicated sentences.** Prepare these in advance, so you can say them quickly as though they were part of a natural conversation. These sentences and words make sense, but many people will not be able to untangle the meaning. Here are a few that you can adapt to other subjects: 'I wouldn't be talking to you about this if I didn't think that I wasn't alone in my views.' (basically means, 'I think we agree.')

    'Money is better than poverty, if only for financial reasons.' (This is utter nonsense, but it still sounds smart. Admit it, you did try decoding it!)

3. **Random questions.** During the middle of the argument, stop and ask the person a question. Be genuinely curious in your delivery. This will likely prompt them to answer the question sincerely, making them forget what they were talking about originally.

Interrupt the argument with, 'Just curious, but are you allergic to any foods?' or 'If you could be one pop-star for a day, who would you be? I was just wondering.'
4. **Create unclear connections.** For example, say 'What you just said reminds me of my father's ex-roommate's friend's daughter, who just adored eating apple pie.' You can make up these connections or trace actual paths to friends or family you know. If you want to trigger mild surprise or a laugh, this is a good tactic to choose.
5. **Information overload.** Start giving a lot of details about a subject and confuse the receiver. For example, if you discuss a plan and your boss does not like it, show him all figures and details. This might put pressure on him and he will get convinced, without you coming across as pushy. Rather, you'll be seen as logical and credible.
6. **Vague words.** These can create wrong or confusing meanings in your receiver's mind. They state a general idea but leave the precise meaning to the receiver's interpretation; so you can blame them for misinterpreting you just in case you have to. Here are a few random examples:
- many: 1,000 or 500 to 1,000
- early: 5 a.m.
- hot: 100 degrees Fahrenheit
- most: 79.9 per cent
- others: business administration students
- poor student: has a 1.6 grade point average (4.0 = A)
- very rich: a millionaire
- soon: 7 p.m., Tuesday

- **The Jedi-Mind trick.** Of course, by far the best method of winning any argument is to have no argument at all. What if, instead of fighting and opposing you at every move, your opponent looked for ways to agree with you? For those of you who aren't familiar with Star Wars, the Jedi Mind Trick refers to the capacity of Jedi Masters to implant thoughts and ideas into the minds of others, convincing them to do what the Jedi wishes because they believe it is their own idea. Assuming, unlike me, you don't actually have superpower telepathic abilities, one way to do this is to give your opponent a self-interested reason to agree with you.

    Find some benefits for the other person in the position that you are advocating and highlight these benefits early on. Steadily, as the idea works its way through their psyche, the strength of their opposition begins to melt away as self-interest takes hold. This is a particularly good one for work disputes.

    Example: two employees, Ally and Nick argue about the best approach to a sales meeting with a client. They can't agree. Then Ally argues that under her approach, half of the work that Nick would have to accomplish under his own proposal might be assigned to a co-worker, with Nick still receiving credit for the effort. Nick suddenly sees the light and even proposes ideas to strengthen Ally's plan. It's the pinnacle of debating without actually debating. It's difficult to pull off, but if you can, it's rather effective. That's all there is to it. Artful, crafty, sly, and just a smidgeon of evil.

Here's a small pool of vague questions and answers for you to use in your next argument/debate with your co-worker:

- 'I want to avoid a rush to judgment.' (We basically don't have all the facts yet.)
- 'More or less', 'kind of', 'sort of', etc.
- 'We must wait until all the facts are in.' (But business executives must act on incomplete information all the time, must they not? This is just another tactic to delay decisions.)
- 'I believe I (or you) need more facts: we don't want to make a decision based on incomplete information, do we?' (This is basically done to delay their say or decision.)
- 'What have you got to lose?' (Real meaning: 'you have virtually no downside and significant upside if you do what *I* want.')
- 'What's the harm in it?' (Similar to the previous one, implying good would likely come by taking action.)
- 'We need to set the record straight' (Real meaning: let me tell you *my* version.)
- 'I hear you.' (Another way of saying, 'I realize you have a different opinion' without agreeing with it one way or another.)
- 'Let me give you the facts.' (Real meaning: 'Here's what *I* want you to believe.')
- 'I'm telling you, that's a fact.' (Real meaning: 'I want you to base your decision on what *I'm* telling you.')
- 'I've thought long and hard.' (This implies that there were many compelling arguments for each side...makes you look considerate of others' opinions.)
- 'You have my support within bounds.' (Real meaning: 'But

you don't have my full support, *as you will learn later.*)
- 'It could go up, it could go down or it could fool us all and go sideways.' (Amazingly, people actually say this stuff. It's an answer that tells you nothing because it covers every possible outcome! Nobody can accuse you of being wrong or lying now.)
- 'This was a very difficult decision.' (Makes you seem empathetic if you're ticking someone off with your decision.)
- 'There were many worthy candidates. This was a very close contest. The people who didn't win *almost won.*' (We've *all* heard this one!)
- 'You make a very good point.' (It's a good, serious response. You're saying it's a good point, but you haven't said you *agree* with it. Smart!)

Five Takeaways for You to Skim Over:

- Office arguments are all about conflicting ideas, goals or desires. Once you manage to tweak all of those in someone's heads, you never have to run away from arguments.
- Arguments done well, can give you everything you want *and beyond.* All you have to do is argue with performed niceness and grace. Don't ever lose your cool or get emotional—that's like you getting stabbed or shot in the forehead during a battle.
- You either charm your opponent through your humour, flattery and emotional story-telling.
- Or, you stand up, tower over them, look them straight in the eye and intimidate them a little with your confidence and expertise (without openly acting like the bad guy, of course.)

- Or better yet, you play mind tricks—you ask them vague questions to confuse them, highlight the gains *they* enjoy through your idea or plan, mimic their body language as well as words, stroke their egos and pretend to listen/empathize before you eventually strike. That way, you weaken them before your final blow. Sneaky? Yes. Useful? Also, yes!